LITSA I. HADJIFOTI

SAINT PAUL

HIS LIFE AND WORK

EDITIONS M. TOUBIS S.A.
ATHENS 2004

The publication of this book would not have been complete without the generous contribution of the photographs of the mosaics of Saint Lydia by Vlasis Tsotsonis. For this I would like to express my warm thanks to his Holiness the Bishop of Philippi, Neapolis and Thasos.
Litsa I. Hadjifoti

© Copyright 2004   MICHAEL TOUBIS PUBLICATIONS S.A.
Nisiza Karela, Koropi, Attiki.
Telephone: +30 210 6029974, Fax: +30 210 6646856
Web Site: http://www.toubis.gr

ISBN: 960-540-557-1

СГА ПАVΛΟ

Saint Paul in Holy Prayer, third quarter of the 4th century, Chilander Monastery, Mount Athos.

The Holy Apostles James and Paul. Wall painting from the cathedral church of the Monastery of St Dionysios, Mount Athos.

CONTENTS

An introduction to Saint Paul 6
Saint Paul, his day and the Greeks 12
The Greek *koine* language 14
The Jews of the Diaspora 15
The representation of Saint Paul in works of art 17
Mission to the Gentiles 22

FIRST MISSION (AD 47-48) **26**
At Salamis in Cyprus 26
At Paphos 30
At Perga 39
At Antioch in Pisida 42

SECOND MISSION (AD 49-52) **45**
On the Road for Troas 46
Samothrace 48
Neapolis (Kavala) 52
Philippi 58
Amphipolis 67
Apollonia 69
Acanthus 69
Thessaloniki 70
Berea 82
Athens 91
Corinth 102

THIRD MISSION (AD 52-56) **112**
Ephesus 112
In Greece Once More 119
Mytilene, Chios, Samos 120
Miletus, Kos, Rhodes 126

FOURTH MISSION (AD 59-61) **132**
The Journey to Rome 132
Melite 134
Rome - The End 136

BIBLIOGRAPHY 142

AN INTRODUCTION TO SAINT PAUL

 hen Ananias, the disciple of the Apostles who lived in the city of Damascus in Syria, saw a vision in which God commanded him to go and find the Straight Road, to a Saul who was at the house of Judas, and to lay his hands upon him to restore his sight, a splendid new chapter was opened in the annals of human history. *"Go, for he is a chosen vessel of Mine to bear My name before Gentiles, kings, and the children of Israel"*, the Lord said to Ananias, and added revealingly: *"For I will show him how many things he must suffer for My name's sake"* (Acts 9:15-16).

Let us, however, take things from the beginning. We are in Tarsus in Cilicia around six or seven years after the birth of Christ. The Assyrians had built this city in the 7th century BC, choosing a very favourable site where the only decent passage across the Taurus Mountains in Asia Minor lies. Its excellent harbour allowed the residents regular commercial and cultural interaction with the people of the eastern Mediterranean.

This resulted in the creation of a university in the city, with the flourishing of education and Greek philosophy under the Romans. It is said that Tarsus is where Cleopatra first met Mark Antony in 41 BC.

One day in the year AD 6 or 7, then, a little boy called Saul was born in Tarsus of Cilicia to Jewish parents of the tribe of Benjamin. Saul would later talk of his hometown with pride: *"I am a Jew from Tarsus, in Cilicia, a citizen of no mean city"* (Acts 21:39). The boy's father was a Roman citizen, suggesting that he may have belonged to the city's upper social ranks. Paul was a tentmaker. It is not clear how many children the family had, although mention is made of a daughter (Acts 23:16).

In Tarsus, as in many other cities of Asia Minor, there was a Jewish community that preserved its customs and traditions, with the synagogue lying at the heart of its cultural and religious life. This is where Saul was taught the history of his ancestors and embraced the zeal by which the Pharisees piously followed the Laws of Moses, as well as the anticipation for the coming of the Messiah who would free the Israelites from Roman rule and return them to their homeland.

Raised with the dynamism of Mosaic Law, and having learnt to distinguish all things Jewish from idolatry and the Gentiles, the child was sent by his parents to Jerusalem to study alongside Gamaliel the Elder, a great rabbi of the day. His became a distinguished expert on Judaic theology and a good jurist. He also acquired an excellent knowledge of the Greek language, literature and philosophy, as can be seen from his later life and work.

Sometime around AD 30, then, Saul, although still young, had developed a strong religious persona and a passionate zeal for his national and religious tradition.

There is no surviving evidence to suggest that he had met Jesus Christ before His Crucifixion and Resurrection. One of Paul's letters does, however, hint at this possibility: *"Even though we have known Christ according to the flesh, yet now we know Him thus no longer."* (2 Corinthians 5: 16). This is not, however, irrefutable evidence.

After the Ascension of Christ and the Pentecost, the religious life of the Christian community of Jerusalem becomes increasingly pronounced. The Apostles preached to the people and announced the resurrection of the dead. The faithful multiplied, miracles happened and the unease and indignation of the Priests and the Secretaries of course increased. They sought explanations for the actions of the Apostles, even reaching the point of physically attacking them so that they would stop preaching that Jesus was the Messiah.

Indeed, at one point some even falsely claimed that they had heard Stephen, one of the seven first deacons, blaspheme against God and Moses. Through a series of procedures, and despite Stephen's own apology, they had him condemned to death by stoning.

It was during this event that Saul first appears as a historical figure. It is clearly stated in the Acts of the Apostles that those who took part in the stoning removed their clothes and lay them down at the feet of a young man named Saul, who was in agreement with this punishment (Acts 7:58-60). Indeed, this is the man who was to prey so intently upon the Church.

Saul became the fear of the Christians. He would intrude without question into their houses and drag the men and women off to prison (Acts 8:3). His mania was so great that

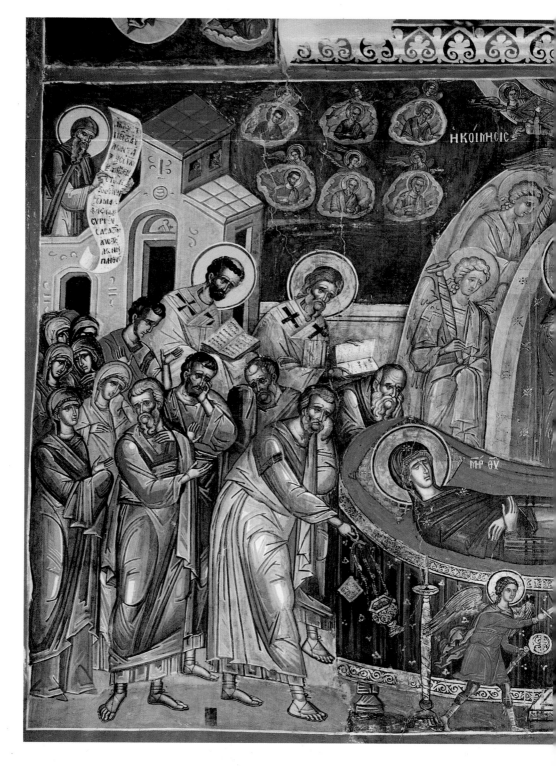

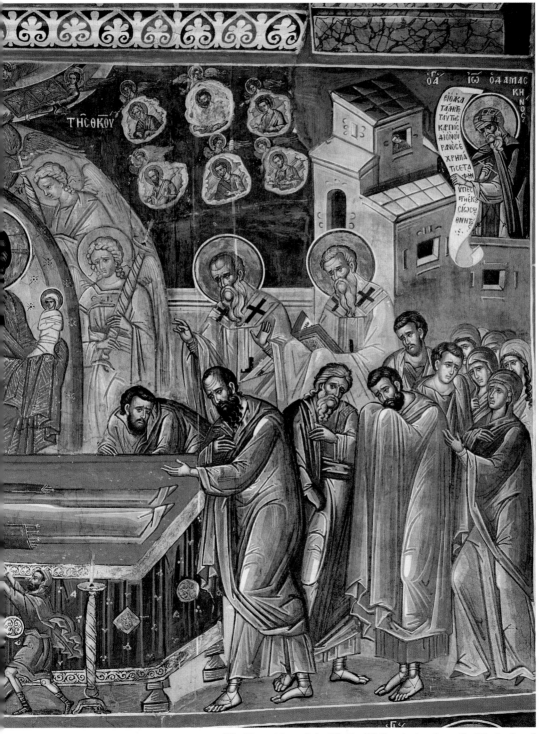

*The Dormition of the Virgin. Wall painting from the Virginal cycle
of the Holy Monastery of St Dionysios. At the feet of the Virgin is St Paul.*

The Bema of St Paul at Berea.

he even requested from the high priest letters to the synagogues of Damascus so that he could go there and remove those faithful to the Nazarene and bring them bound to Jerusalem.

Damascus was an ancient city. It is mentioned in the tablets of Tel-el Amarna from Egypt as among the cities that Tuthmosis III ruled. Egyptians, Israelites, Chaldeans, Syrians and Persians had all been masters of Damascus, famous for its trade, until 333 BC when Alexander the Great conquered Syria. After him the Hellenistic period begins for Damascus, with new rulers the Seleucids. After them came the Romans and later the Byzantines.

Many Greeks settled in Damascus around 90 BC, exercising a strong cultural influence on the native population. A city that was wholly Greek grew alongside Aramaic Damascus. This flourishing period did not last for long. The Nabataeans settled in Damascus in 85 BC and in 67 BC came the Romans, who made a Roman province of Syria. The Nabataeans retook it in AD 37, remaining there until AD 54. This is around the time that Paul arrived in the city. A small chapel survives near the Bab Sharqi Gate. The silt deposits give the impression that it is an underground construction, and it is made up of two sections, one of which is a church dedicated to the Holy Cross and that was later dedicated to Saint Ananias. It is well preserved and is connected with the event that followed.

We find ourselves in around AD 33. Saul and his entourage are on the road to Damascus when, suddenly, a strong light strikes him to the ground. Saul falls down and hears an otherworldly voice ask him, *"Saul, Saul, why are you persecuting Me?" "Who are You, Lord?"* Saul stammered. *"I am Jesus, whom you are persecuting,"* the voice of the Lord was heard again, and added *"Arise and go into the city, and you will be told what you must do".* Saul's fellow travellers listened dumbfounded to the dialogue with the unknown voice. Concerned, they saw Saul getting up with difficulty. His eyes were open, yet he could not see! They helped him continue on his road and finally arrived at the house of Judas on the Straight Road, where Ananias, commanded by the Lord, found him three days after the events on the road to Damascus.

Ananias lay his hands on the blind Saul and, by a miracle, things that looked like scales fell from his eyes. Saul had regained his sight. He immediately converted and was baptised in the name of Christ and began to preach with strength and passion that He is the Messiah.

It is not difficult for one to imagine the surprise of all those who had previously known Saul as a persecutor and tyrant of the Disciples of Christ and, naturally, of the anger and fury of the Jews when everyone learnt of his conversion. His old comrades plotted to kill him, but the disciples let him down over the walls of Damascus in a basket and helped him escape.

"The Baptism of St Paul",
painted miniature manuscript, 11th century,
Vatopedion Monastery, Mount Athos.

SAINT PAUL,
HIS DAY AND THE GREEKS

ust like in a myth, the former terrifying and relentless persecutor Saul, who *"is also called Paul"* (Acts 13: 9) - the name by which he went down in history, becomes the persecuted in the name of Jesus Christ. However this transformation may be characterised, either in scientific terms or as a miracle, it is an undeniable fact that it was to be a major event for the whole of humanity, and for Hellenism in particular. Above all, the Apostle to the Gentiles, one of the greatest personages to have been born on Earth, is beyond doubt the enlightener of the Greeks, and for this reason the modern-day Church of Greece claims him as a founder.

Paul travelled repeatedly throughout Greece and founded local churches, maintaining an undying interest in the disciples that he left behind. It is also well known that five of his Epistles are addressed to Greeks. Two are to churches in Central Greece (1 and 2 Corinthians) and another two are addressed to the churches of Greek cities in Asia Minor, i.e. to Greeks (Ephesians and Colossians). The epistle to Philemon is probably addressed to a Greek church, whilst another three are addressed to the heads of Greek churches: two to Timothy (1 and 2) and one to Titus (the former was the first Bishop of Ephesus and the latter the first Bishop of Gortyn in Crete).

It is also not possible to overlook the fact that the Galatians of Asia Minor, to whom Paul addressed one of his Epistles, were Hellenised and that the Epistle to the Romans was written in Greek.

More than anything, the Bible was preached in Greek and the whole of the New Testament was originally written in Greek. Also noteworthy is the fact that the work of the Apostle Paul was recorded and saved by the Greek Gospel writer Luke, whom the Apostle characteristically and eloquently describes as *"Luke the beloved physician"* (Coll. 4:14). Moreover, no other Christian church can so persuasively portray the Apostle as its founder, as the Orthodox Church of Greece can. Of course this was after the Church of Sion, i.e. the church of Jerusalem, which was based upon the Cross of the Martyr and the blood of Jesus Christ.

Finally, it is characteristic that the Apostle Paul was called upon to do his work and calling by Christ Himself, who realised that even though he had been His relentless persecutor, all that Paul wanted, as St John Chrysostom observed in one of his homilies on Saint Paul, was Jesus's love.

Central panel in a triptych showing the embrace of Peter and Paul. Cretan workshop, 3rd quarter 16th century.

THE GREEK *KOINE* LANGUAGE

he relationship between the Apostle Paul and the Greeks discussed above was of course neither by chance or incidental. The geographical spread of the Greeks from ancient times until the age of Jesus meant that the Greek language had evolved into one common language, the *koine*, which in its broadest form was used in the daily communication of the Greeks of the Diaspora. At the same time, it became the mother tongue of those people born in the communities that were created in these regions.

The strength and the prestige of Athenian democracy meant that use of the Attic dialect held strong amongst most Greeks as the common language of communication, to the degree that in the mid-4th century Phillip II, King of Macedon, established it as the official language of Macedonian government and diplomacy. The *koine* evolved with some local variations, without ever ceasing to be overwhelmingly uniform. It is an exceptionally rich language with terms that render profound concepts, making possible penetrating analyses and highly intellectual expressions. In other words, it is a perfect means of expression for teaching the Bible. Elements of the *koine* can be found in the Books of the Bible, such as the translation of the Septuagint, the New Testament, the Epistles, and other documents dating from the late 4th century BC to the 8th century AD.

Despite the decline of such centres, mainly those in Greece such as Athens and Corinth, the cultural cache of Hellenism in the years of Jesus and the Apostles was exceptionally high. One might say that it was ready, willing to accept and to absorb and to become the mechanism by which the Teachings of the Nazarene were to spread. The inscription to the 'Unknown Gods' that Paul would later see in Athens is undeniable proof of this position.

Under Ptolemy II Philadelphus (285-246 BC) seventy-two Greek-speaking Jews began to translate the Pentateuch (the Torah, or the first five Books of the Old Testament, and the Apocrypha) into this Hellenistic *koine*, as it was used in Alexandria in Egypt. This became known as the Septuagint.

This is the earliest translation of the Old Testament, a splendid effort and a work of great theological, philological and historical importance, completed in the middle of the 2nd century BC. It is said that the translators worked on the island of Pharos, and that a copy of their work must have been kept in the famous Library of Alexandria, which was later burnt down.

The Christian church used the Old Testament by following the example of the Apostles, in particular the Apostle Paul, who made much reference to it in his Epistles, e.g. in Hebrews and Ephesians.

THE JEWS OF THE DIASPORA

he movement of the Israelites around the Mediterranean during the two centuries before Christ must not be underestimated. During the Hellenistic period Judaism spread throughout the whole known world. Flavius Josephus, a Jewish historian active in the time of Christ, notes that his contemporary the Greek geographer Strabo argued that *"the Judaic nation has spread to every city"*. Another Jewish philosopher, Philo of Alexandria, included among the places where Israelites had settled Greek areas such as: Thessaly, Macedonia, Aitolia, Attica, Argos, Corinth, the Peloponnese and the islands of the Aegean. Even Sparta had a Jewish community. The Jews of the Diaspora lived in their own communities, although this was not imposed upon them by the Greeks or the Romans. They had the right not to participate in the idolatrous religions and some of them even managed to purchase the title of Roman citizen, as the Apostle Paul's father did. They were in close contact with the Greeks, knew, spoke and wrote the Greek language, expressed an interest in Greek religion and philosophical trends, and were, of course, a little influenced by all this, something which distinguished them from the communities in Judea. Philo of Alexandria, a Jewish philosopher and jurist, is a typical example. He admired Plato and, with exceptional skill, managed to combine Greek thought and Judaic tradition. Yet, the Greek-speaking Jews never ceased to follow their true religious tradition and were never converted. On the contrary, it appears that not a few idolaters were converted either wholly or in part to Judaism, many of whom were women.

The statue of the Apostle in front of the Basilica of St Paul "outside the walls" of Rome.

THE REPRESENTATION OF SAINT PAUL IN WORKS OF ART

aint Paul was a favoured subject matter in Orthodox and Christian art as a whole, from its beginnings in the early Christian period, although in the centuries before Constantine the Great the representation of "sleeping" figures, scenes of martyrdom and death in general were not common. His teachings were also greatly loved and his own presence resulted in them becoming spread over a large area of the Mediterranean basin.

One of the earliest representations of Saint Paul is believed to have been preserved in the Catacombs of Domitilla in Rome, which dates to around 348. The figure represented here has a long - we might describe it as elongated - face, large forehead and bald patch, hooked nose and a beard that is not so long. This work introduces the type by which Saint Paul would most commonly be represented over the centuries until our days, particularly in Orthodox art. These characteristics spread from early Christian times until the Byzantine and even post-Byzantine years. This image was codified in the words of the Monk Dionysus from Fourna in Agrapha, Evrytania in his work "An Interpretation of Painted Art": *"Paul bald, quivering, quite hoary,*

holding his 14 letters all rolled and bound together".

As a synecdoche, these fourteen small scrolls are often substituted by one, the literary work of the Apostle, the essence of his teaching and expressing his constant interest in the congregation of his Lord.

In Western European art the sword is a typical motif in the representation of Saint Paul. This feature symbolises his execution and beheading as well as the dynamism of his teaching, which sliced away thousands of non-believers from idolatry. A typical example is the statue of him in front of the splendid Basilica of Saint Paul "outside the walls" of Rome.

Among the oldest and most characteristic representations of St Paul are the symbolic relief figures on sarcophagi known typically as the 'sarcophagi passionis', i.e. of the passion, because they show either the martyrdom of Christ or the martyrdom of Saints Peter and Paul. Such monuments date from the mid-fourth to the mid-fifth century and are found in Italy and France. Typical examples are the sarcophagus of Junius Bassus from AD 359 (Grotte Vaticane, Rome) and the sarcophagus of St Magdalene from AD 360-370 (Toulon region), as well as a sarcophagus from the catacombs of St Sebastian in Rome, dating to *ca* AD 370.

Of particular interest are two early works that represent Saint Paul with a full head of hair. One is a fragment from a relief sculpture of the 4th or 5th century now in a Museum in Italy, with Peter and Paul facing each other. The other is an ivory plaque with Saint Paul represented in frontal full-figure holding the Bible in his right hand.

Of the wonderful mosaic representations, mention should be made of those in the Palatine Chapel in Palermo, Sicily dating to the 12th century, which are among the finest examples of this art. In the Palatine Chapel, St Paul is shown being baptised in Damascus by Ananias, talking with Jews in the synagogue and at the moment when he and Peter embraced during their meeting at the site of the Three Taverns in Rome.

Of the surviving wall paintings with representations of Saint Paul, mention should be made of a fragment of a wall painting showing the embrace between SS Peter and Paul (1170-1180) in the Cathedral church of the Holy Monastery of Vatopedion on Mount Athos. We should also note the work in the church of Protatos at Karyes on Mount Athos by M. Panselinos (1290), that in the cell of Rabdouchos just outside Karyes (early 13th century) and, finally, the wall painting in the Holy Monastery

The catacombs of St Sebastian, Rome.

Saint Paul in between Saints Andrew and Peter.
Work by Theophanes Strelitza-Batha (2nd half 6th century).
Wall painting from the Holy Monastery of Stavronikita, Mount Athos.

of Stavronikitas on Mount Athos. In this work Paul is shown between the Apostles Andrew and Peter (first half of the 16th century), a work by Theophanes the Cretan.

Of course, the number of portable icons of St Paul throughout the length and breadth of the Orthodox world is immeasurable. Among these, mention should be made of the very ancient icons of the Holy Monastery of St Catherine on Mt Sinai, and the works of great Orthodox icon painters, such as Zorzis and Angelos as well as modern artists such as Fotis Kontoglou. There is a similar number of miniatures and

"The embrace of Peter and Paul". Section of a wall painting (ca 1170-1180), Holy Vatopedion Monastery, Mount Athos.

other works of art, among which we can include a double-sided talisman from the 13th century in the Holy Monastery of Vatopedion.

In addition to representations of his beheading or the embrace with St Peter - which is the most characteristic representation of the celebration of their memory on the same day of 29 June - Paul is also portrayed in more complex representations. These include the Ascension (Sinai), the Dormition of the Virgin (Holy Monastery of Stavronikitas) and the Groping of Thomas (private collection of John Latsis). A number of works by Dionysios of Fourna represents events and miracles in Paul's life, such as "Paul in a basket hung over the walls escapes from the Jews" (with the escape from Jerusalem in a basket), "Paul blinds Bar-Jesus the sorcerer", "Paul exorcising the girl filled with the spirit of Python" and other works.

Saints Peter and Paul (mid 14th century). Holy Monastery of St Catherine, Sinai.

MISSION TO THE GENTILES

fter the events of Damascus Paul stayed in Jerusalem for a while. Here, with the passing of time and his communication with the Apostles, he managed to persuade them of his conversion. The Acts of the Apostles say that, in order to escape from the Greek-speaking Jews who threatened to annihilate him because he attempted to talk to them about the teachings of Christ, he was sent from Jerusalem to Caesarea and Tarsus, where he rested for a while. Two or three years must have passed until Paul, with the help of Barnabas, was able to leave his homeland and travel to Antioch. *"So it was that for a whole year they assembled with the church and taught a great many people. And the disciples were the first called Christians in Antioch"* (Acts 11:26). This was followed by the death of James, the brother of John, the imprisonment of Peter (who escaped with the assistance of an angel), as well as famine in Judea, where Paul and Barnabas were sent to help). Their return to Antioch also marks the beginning of Paul's Apostolic career. As we shall see below, he has been justly described as a result of this work as the "Apostle to the Gentiles".

Antioch was the centre of the Kingdom of the Selucids. It was founded in 300 BC by Seleucus I Nikatorus, an old general of Alexander the Great, on an excellent site from a military and trading view on the left bank of the River Orontis. From the time of Antiochus IV (175-163 BC) it was made up of four districts each with a separate surround wall, and was thus called Tetrapolis by Strabo. The palace was located on an islet in the river.

In 64 BC it came under Roman control and became the seat of the Roman garrison of Syria, later emerging as one of the earliest and most important centres of Christianity. Antioch is where Saint Paul commenced his mission and he often used the city as his base. Many of the first martyrs to the faith of Jesus Christ came from Antioch, which in the fourth century was the most important city of the East. It had a strong church, and the classics and theological studies flourished here. At some point the theological disputes of the fourth century resulted in a church schism, and Nestorianism emerged in the fifth century. The great earthquake of 526 is said to have cost the lives of 250,000 people and the city was not able to recover its old glory. Its numerous mosaic floors of exceptional artistic quality, dating mainly from the Roman period and also later, such as the mosaic floor of the suburb of Daphne from the late fifth century with its representation of a 'map' of the city, were completely lost. We have some snippets of information in the work of St John Chrysostom and Libanius in his oration on Antioch (AD 360). The city's port was Seleucid Pieria, at the mouth of the River Orontis.

The Acts of the Apostles informs us that there were many prophets and teachers in the Church of Antioch in those days, such as Barnabas, Simon who was also called Niger, Lucius of Cyrene, Manaen who was associated with Herod the tetrach and Paul. One day, as they were ministering to the Lord, fasting and praying, the Holy Spirit said to them *"Now separate to Me Barnabas and Saul for the work to which I have called them"*. All those present continued until they had done fasting and praying and then blessed the two men and bid them farewell (Acts 3:1-3).

Thus began the missionary work of the Apostle Paul, his total of four tours during which he came into contact with many people in many parts of the then known world. He was to preach the Word of God, to baptise, found Churches and to fight for their dominance.

The Acts of the Apostles close with Saint Paul's sojourn in Rome. From the Pastoral Epistles, various church authors and the general narrative of the Acts, it is believed that Paul visited Spain and undertook yet another journey to the East: Asia Minor, Crete, Macedonia, Illyria, ending up in Rome, were he was beheaded by Nero (AD 68). The Missions of Paul are presented in the chronological order in which they were undertaken. It is not possible to ascribe precise dates to them, although the dates given here are drawn from many years of research by specialists, who have taken into consideration theological historical, archaeological, astronomical and other factors.

It is said that he covered over 4,000 kilometres during his Missions, passing over sea and land, rivers, mountains and deserts. He suffered from thirst, hunger, injustices, persecution, stoning, imprisonment and lack of sleep. He visited almost all the cities of Asia Minor, the most important in Greece, went to Rome twice and perhaps even reached as far as Spain.

It is said that his origins, his education and his status as a Roman citizen in an era when, thanks to Roman domination, there was free travel through the countries of the Mediterranean, all made it easier for him to accomplish his giant, inestimable work.

It is also said that his knowledge of the Greek language played a decisive role in his ability to communicate and that the existence of synagogues in many cities enabled him to find a starting point for his work at each place.

It is moreover said that he had the ability to speak to people through their own spiritual, cultural and general interests and knew how to choose the companions for his journeys. He had the ability to set his associates apart. Some of these continued his work as Bishops, such as Timothy in Ephesus and Titus in Crete.

But, of course, nothing happens by chance alone. Those who claim that History is a set of coincidences are arguing in vain. Paul was not a typical, common man. He was a great personage, a talented man with many qualities, a broad education and a general awareness. All this, of course, makes up the external factors, the human ones. There is also one other factor: that Paul embraced with a

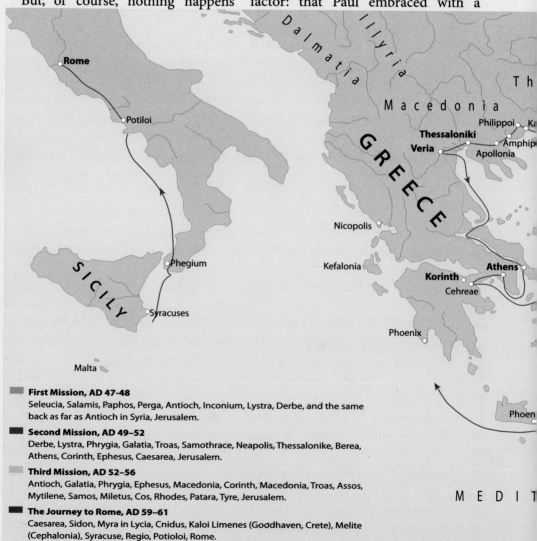

First Mission, AD 47-48
Seleucia, Salamis, Paphos, Perga, Antioch, Inconium, Lystra, Derbe, and the same back as far as Antioch in Syria, Jerusalem.

Second Mission, AD 49-52
Derbe, Lystra, Phrygia, Galatia, Troas, Samothrace, Neapolis, Thessalonike, Berea, Athens, Corinth, Ephesus, Caesarea, Jerusalem.

Third Mission, AD 52-56
Antioch, Galatia, Phrygia, Ephesus, Macedonia, Corinth, Macedonia, Troas, Assos, Mytilene, Samos, Miletus, Cos, Rhodes, Patara, Tyre, Jerusalem.

The Journey to Rome, AD 59-61
Caesarea, Sidon, Myra in Lycia, Cnidus, Kaloi Limenes (Goodhaven, Crete), Melite (Cephalonia), Syracuse, Regio, Potioloi, Rome.

passion and absolute devotion the command to travel and teach all the Gentiles. He did not stop until the moment that the Roman soldier's sword cut short the thread of his earthly existence.

There is, however, yet one other component. This does not depend upon coincidences, abilities or opportunities. It does not depend on the qualities of one individual, on a human being. It is the choice of God, Holy Grace, the divine calling that commanded Paul to *"bear My name before Gentiles, kings, and the children of Israel"*. It is, finally, his identification with the love of Christ, who as he claims in his Epistle to the Galatians: *"I have been crucified with Christ; it is no longer I who live, but Christ lives in me"* (Gal. 2:20).

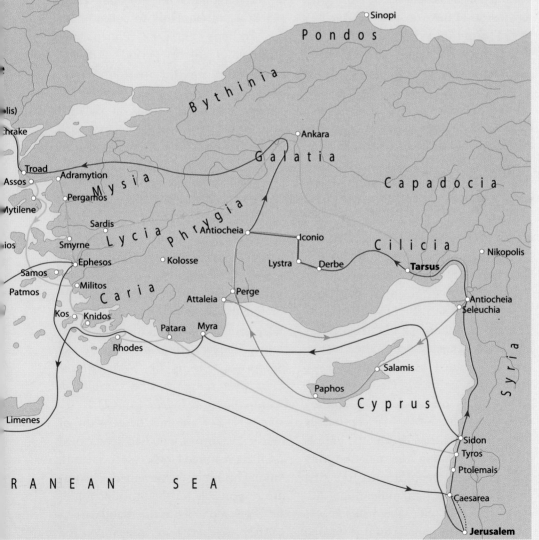

FIRST MISSION (AD 47-48)
AT SALAMIS IN CYPRUS

aul and Barnabas, sent by the Holy Spirit as the Acts of the Apostles (13:4) tell us, began to put into practice the task for which they had been chosen. They disembarked at Seleucia, a port bustling with life, quickly found a boat and set sail in a westerly direction towards Cyprus, the shores of which were not so far away. Their first stop was Salamis, north of today's Famagusta. Both have been captured by the Turks for many years now, and are today located in the Turkish Cypriot "state". But, we shall return to the Year of Our Lord 47.

The city of Salamis is an ancient one. Tradition says that is was built by Teucer, the son of Telamon of Salamis in Attica who was the brother of Ajax. Teucer was a hero of the Trojan War, and reached these shores after having been persecuted by his father, or so Strabo tells us in his Geography (14. 16,3). Lying on ancient sea routes, rich in minerals and exceptionally fertile, Cyprus has been the Apple of Discord among the neighbouring Mediterranean peoples since the first centuries of the first millennium BC. From 707-669 BC the island was under Assyrian rule. Later it passed

to the Egyptians for 25 years (570-545 BC), subsequently to come under the Persians and the Phoenicians. Throughout all this period, until 411 BC, Salamis was the most important city on Cyprus.

The Royal Necropolis at Salamis dates to the years when the Assyrians were settled on the island. Here we can see an impressive show of strength combined with eastern wealth. The structures, which the public is generally unaware of, here occupy around 6,000 square metres. In one tomb, number 8, which dates to 530 BC, silver obols of King Euelthon have been found, the first examples of coinage on Cyprus. As for Euelthon, whose name appears on these coins, he is the earliest historical figure, Teucer's first descendant. As Herodotus tells us, he *dedicated the remarkable censer in the Corinithian treasure-house at Delphi*" (4, 162).

In 411 BC another descendant of Teucer, Evagoroas, who had been exiled in Cilicia, restored Greek rule to Salamis. Among his many achievements, he was also responsible for the introduction of the Greek alphabet to the island.

After the death of Alexander the

Great Salamis came under the rule of Nikokreon, another distinguished native of the city. In the decade 306-295 BC, just a short distance from the Royal Necropolis and prehistoric Enkomi, the monument known as the Cenotaph of Nikokreon was built. This monument is unique among its kind in Cyprus, and an artificial tumulus was built upon it in the 3rd century BC. The tumulus enclosed a rectangular podium built of small bricks, upon which sixteen clay busts of members of the royal family had been set. Other objects were also found, which subsequently remained in the fire with the dead body of Nikokreon, who chose to kill himself rather than hand over the city to Ptolemy I Soter. Sometime later Paphos was to emerge as the island's administrative centre, which among its other advantages is located nearer to the Egyptian coast and to Alexandria.

Of the surviving monuments of ancient Salamis worthy of particular mention are the restored temple of Olympian Zeus at the south edge of the Theatre, which dates to the first century AD and the Gymnasium, built upon an older Hellenistic structure. In the 2nd century AD a palaestra was also built here, surrounded by four colonnades, Baths and the remains of the Roman forum. The excavations that had been started in Salamis by the Cyprus Department of Antiquities came to a halt with the Turkish invasion of 1974.

In the Year of Our Lord 47, then, Paul and Barnabas along with John Mark disembark at Salamis and go to the synagogues where they preach the Word of the Lord. They literally went all over the island preaching the Word of the Lord in the synagogues of the Jews, until one day they reached Paphos, on the west coast of Cyprus.

The theatre at Salamis, prior to 1974.

The ruins of ancient Salamis in occupied Famagusta, prior to 1974.

AT PAPHOS

aphos is famous as the birthplace of Aphrodite. According to Greek mythology, the goddess rose from the foam of the waves at a spot just outside the city, near today's site of the Petra tou Romiou (the Roman's Rock, also known as Aphrodite's Rock). The city is famed for its worship of the goddess.

The city that was visited by the Apostles was not the one that the Arcadian hero Agapenor founded after the Trojan War, as Homer records (*Odyssey* I, 362-363). This original city was located around sixteen kilometres to the east of today's Paphos, which is now known as Old Paphos (Palaipaphos). In 321 BC Nikokles (325–310 BC) the last king of the old city of Paphos, moved his kingdom to the site that today extends to the little port of modern Paphos, . The old city of Palaipaphos is today known as Kouklia, and it continued to be the

The Odeion of Paphos

leading centre of worship on Cyprus with the most important sanctuary of Aphrodite in the known ancient world.

Archaeological excavations began here in 1888, and have demonstrated the continued existence of a settlement on this site from around the middle of the first millennium BC to the late Middle Ages. From the end of the 8th century it was protected by an enclosure wall that was destroyed in 498 BC, during the Ionian revolt against the Persians. It was rebuilt for the last time during the second half of the 4th century BC.

The original sanctuary of Aphrodite consisted of a temple with a surround wall made from giant limestone blocks, and a sanctuary hall in its north-west section. In the north of the sanctuary there are remains of a later Roman temple. There was no cult statue in the sanctuary temple, just a conical stone that represented fertility. The worship of Aphrodite in Paphos was aniconic and is believed to be associated with the worship of the oriental goddess Astarte.

The Nobel Laureate George Seferis visited the temple of Aphrodite in November 1953 and wrote the poem 'In the Goddess' Name I Summon You'.

The Paphos that the Apostles visited was the city founded by Nikokles. This city served as the capital of Cyprus for a long time and was its trade and

Dionysios and Jocaste,
mosaic from the House of Diònysios.

The archaeological site
of Old Paphos.

economic centre until the 4th century AD when its place was taken by Salamis, which was later named Constantia. It flourished particularly during the Roman period, when it had the right to mint its own coinage.

Among the city's most important monuments are the theatre, which dates to the 3rd century BC, the Odeion, constructed in the early 2nd century BC, the Agora and the Asclepieion, of the same date as the Odeion. These last two structures were destroyed by earthquakes in the first half of the 4th century, and the capital was then transferred to Salamis. The Emperor Justinian was later to display a great interest in Paphos, and Cyprus in general. The city later suffered greatly under successive Arab raids, finally falling into decline under Frankish rule.

The monuments that are of particular interest to visitors are the four Roman villas with excellently preserved mosaics of high craftsmanship and the cemetery known as the Tombs of the Kings.

The most impressive of the Roman villas is that known as the House of Dionysus, so named because the god acts as central figure in the decoration of its mosaic floors. The villa dates to the 2nd century AD and must have belonged to an eminent and cultivated resident of the city. It was discovered by chance in 1962 during agricultural work and appears to have been built on the site of an earlier house. This villa was very spacious, with dimensions of 2,000 square metres, of which the mosaic floors took up 556 square metres. The external walls and roof of the building have been restored so as to protect the mosaics.

A remarkable world that strikes a balance between the extraordinary reality of the well-made and well-preserved mosaics and the extraordinary poetic world conjured up by the mythological subject matter of the mosaics. We see the Four Seasons, Narcissus, Apollo and Daphne,

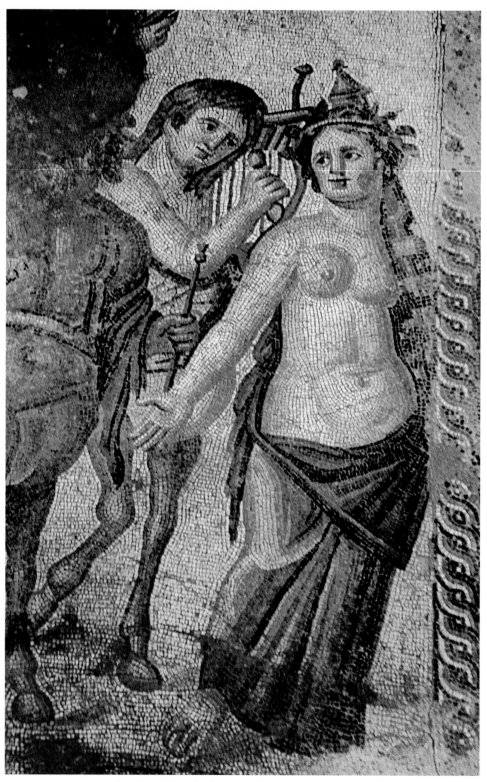

"Apollo and Daphne", mosaic from the House of Aion.

Above: St Kyriaki the Chrysospiliotissa. Thirty metres to the west of the church is the marble column from which it is believed that St Paul was tied and whipped during his visit to Cyprus in AD 45.

Left: Catacomb of Saint Solomoni.

Ganymede and the Eagle, the Triumph of Dionysus, and much more, all framed by leaves, branches, animals, meanders, braids and rhomboids. A riot of colours, fantasy and mythological and artistic lore that the owner's financial wellbeing left to history.

The other Roman houses with splendid mosaic floors are the House of Theseus, the largest Roman building on Cyprus with dimensions of 120 x 80 metres and over 100 rooms, the House of Aion, perhaps the residence of the Roman Proconsul, and the House of Orpheus.

A little beyond Fabrikas hill, immediately after the entrance to the city, are two 'catacombs'. The one on the right (west) is that of Saint Lambrinos whilst the one on the left (east) is that of Saint Solomoni.

Underground tombs cut into the rock are found in the area of the National Guard Barracks. These date to the late 4th century BC, although their purpose is not entirely clear. The north wall lies a little to the north and the cemetery is located beyond this. A cluster of graves lies very near to the wall, two of which have been excavated and are known as the Painted Graves because of the wall paintings in their antechambers.

The visitor will surely be amazed by the number and size as well as the monumental construction of the Tombs of the Kings, which lie in the north of the cemetery of south Paphos. Kings were certainly not buried here, but the magnitude of the tombs is so great that tradition could attribute them only to kings.

The area of the Tombs of the Kings was in use as a cemetery from the 3rd century BC, and it also later functioned as a place of refuge for the early Christians during the years of persecution. In the Middle Ages various intruders settled in some of the tombs, altering their orientation and original architecture. In 1977 the Department of Antiquities of the Republic of Cyprus undertook systematic excavations, aware that these monuments were unique on the island. The temple-like facades of the tombs are reminiscent of those at Vergina in northern Greece. Many scholars comment that this should not be surprising, giving the great Macedonian influence on the Paphians during the Hellenistic period. The Tombs of the Kings are large funeral tombs, which open up onto peristyle courtyards, i.e. with columns on all sides. They were built by being carved directly into the rock. The columns are connected by an architrave, above which is an entablature that was also carved from the rock, with triglyphs and metopes. Tomb no 4 is one of the best preserved, and is accessible via a little road with steps.

The Roman Governor of Cyprus when Paul and Barnabas reached the island was the Proconsul Sergius Paulus, a man known for his discretion and moderation. With him was a Jewish pseudo-prophet, Bar-Jesus, whose name meant 'Elymas the sorcerer'. Sergius Paulus invited the Apostles so that he could hear their message and be informed of their teachings. The sorcerer did everything that he could to prevent this. Then Paul, filled with the Holy Spirit, turned to him with a crushing look, said: *"O full of all deceit and fraud, you son of the devil, you enemy of all righteousness, will you not cease perverting the straight ways of the Lord? And now indeed, the hand of the Lord is upon you, and you shall be blind, not seeing the sun for a time"*. At which moment the sorcerer was shrouded by mist and darkness, groping around for someone to lead him along.

Overawed by all that had happened and also by all that he had heard about the teachings of Christ, the Roman proconsul accepted his faith in Him. This event was one of the most significant in Cypriot history. It is particularly impressive because Sergius Paulus was a Roman citizen and high-ranking government official. His conversion to Christianity marked the beginning of the new religion's penetration into the Roman administration. This act was to find many followers in the near future, but it would also be subject to relentless persecution by the Roman emperors.

"The Tombs of the Kings", giant burial chambers in the north section of the necropolis of Paphos.

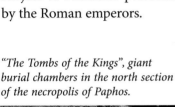

The Hellenistic gates at Perga.

AT PERGA

fter leaving Paphos they went to Perga in Pamphilia, a fine trading city on the road that ran through Cilicia in the direction of Pisidia. The city spread out along the foothills of an expansive hill, in between the rivers Kestros and Katarraktis. It seems that the first inhabitants settled in this region after the Trojan War, and tradition holds that the city was founded by the prophets Mopsos, Calchas and Archilochus. Much later, it was allied to the Athenians during the Peloponnesian War, although from the middle of the fourth century it disappears into obscurity for many years.

When in 334 BC Alexander the Great was marching southwards in a bid to take Pamphylia, then under Persian yoke, Perga had no fortress walls. Its famous walls, which are still kept in very good condition today at almost their original height, were built later in the years of Antiochus III. They had a fine marble decoration, fitted with niches and statues.

In 218 BC Perga came under Seleucid control, under which it flourished greatly. In 188 BC it passed into the domination of Pergamon, until being conquered by the Romans. Under the Romans this Pamphylian city was to witness a new, second phase of cultural and commercial growth.

In the last quarter of the 2nd century BC there lived in Perga a very splendid women, Plancia Magna, a priestess of Artemis and sister of M. Plancius Varus, ruler of Bithynia. Plancia Magna had a number of impressive buildings built and she was very influential in the growth and construction of the city. She came from a distinguished family and her tomb has been discovered outside the city walls, to the east of the formal city gates, which were built into the wall to the south of the Hellenistic gates.

The theatre, with a seating capacity of around 15,000 is one of the city's most important monuments and is a typical example of this type of structure in Asia Minor as it developed in the Roman period. A little further down is the Stadium, which is also extremely large. It was built around the same time as the theatre and has a similar seating capacity. Like the theatre, it was later converted into an arena. Both these monuments are located outside the walls.

The Hellenistic gates of Perga are still imposing even today, thanks to their two circular towers that were built with exceptional craftsmanship. Behind these towers Plancia Magna had a butterfly-shaped courtyard built. This courtyard was enclosed by a wall

The theatre at Perga (2nd century AD). It had a seating capacity of 15,000 and its facade was decorated with relief sculpture.

with niches in which stood statues of the city's founders, the emperor and his wife. Some of these statues were found in their original positions during the excavations. Also impressive are the streets of Perga, which were lined by stoas with shops. There was a large Agora, or Forum, located between the older and newer towers, a magnificent palaestra, most likely a work dedicated to the Emperor Claudius by Julius Cortunus, a large Nymphaeum decorated with the statues of Artemis Pergaia, Septimus Severus, Caracula and Julia Domna. Today's visitor can also see the Baths, wells and the Acropolis in the far north.

The existence of two Christian basilicas, most likely dating to the 4th century and built with isodomic masonry is characteristic. The first basilica has a transverse aisle in its east, which was in the form of a rectangle and a butterfly-shaped apse. The second basilica also had a transept aisle, which protruded, and was five-aisled with colonnades along the long sides projecting into the transept aisle. Paul's visit to the region led to the early acceptance of the teachings of the Nazarene and the creation of one of the oldest centres of Christendom.

The walls of Perga.

IN ANTIOCH OF PISIDA

hen Paul and his party left Perga they made their way to Antioch of Pisida, but without John who left them and returned to Jerusalem.

This city of Antioch lay near the borders of Pisida with Phrygia and had become a Roman colony in the years of Augustus, flourishing in the early Christian years. A significant number of coins and the remains of a number of buildings survive, including an early Christian basilica.

On the Sabbath Paul and his party went to the synagogue and quietly observed the reading of the Law of the Prophets. The rulers of the synagogue then invited them to speak for the good of the people. Paul stood up and, motioning with his hand, began to narrate the story of the Israelites up until the time of John the Baptist, and the crucifixion and resurrection of Christ. *"And we declare to you glad tidings - that promise which was made to the fathers God has fulfilled for us their children, in that He has raised up Jesus. As it is also written in the second Psalm: 'You are My Son. Today I have begotten You'. And that He raised Him from the dead, no more to return to corruption."* And Paul continued: *"Therefore let it be known to you, brethren, that through this Man is preached to you the forgiveness of sins; and by Him everyone who believes is justified from all things which you could not be justified by the law of Moses. Beware therefore, lest what has been spoken in the prophets comes upon you: 'behold, you despisers. Marvel and perish! For I work a work in your days. A work which you will by no means believe, though one were to declare it to you'."*

The passion of Paul's words made an impression, and the Gentiles, as they were leaving the synagogue of the Jews, asked the Apostles to return the next Saturday to continue preaching to them. Then many Jews and proselytes followed Paul and Barnabas, who continued to talk to them of the grace of God.

On the next Sabbath almost the whole city gathered to hear the Word of the Lord. But the Jews were disturbed by this and kept interrupting with objections. At some point Paul and Barnabas grew bold and answered them that the Word of the Lord must be heard by them, but since they were not worthy of hearing it they would turn instead to the Gentiles.

Many did believe, and the Word of the Lord spread everywhere. The Jews were unable to stay calm and forced Paul and Barnabas to abandon their city. The Apostles were pleased, however, because the seed of the Word of the Lord had been sown.

From Antioch in Pisida they went to Inconium, a fine trading city built at a height of 1000 metres. Inconium was the capital of Lycaonia, a land of central Asia Minor, to the north of the Taurus mountain range, in between Pisida, Phrygia and Cappadocia. It passed from Alexander the Great to the Seleucids, then to the Attalids and in 133 BC to the Romans. In later years it was renamed Karamania, from the city of Karaman, the ancient Laranda. Just like the other important cities of Lycaonia (Laodiceia, Lystra, etc.), Inconium was built at a point traversed by one of the most important Roman roads, which ended at the River Euphrates. This fact meant that people from many different ethnic backgrounds (Greeks, Jews, Armenians, etc.) resided in Inconium in the Roman period. Inconium is thought to be one of the world's oldest human settlements, and excavations in one part of the city have proved the existence of human settlement here in the third millennium BC. It is worth noting that in 1958 a Neolithic settlement dating to around 7,000 BC was discovered at Catal Huyuk, around fifty metres south-west of Inconium. With the construction of the Constantinople-Baghdad railway line in 1826 and until 1923 Inconium was the most important city of central Asia Minor. Of course, one cannot omit mentioning that not only did it grow into a leading centre of Christendom,

producing important Bishops who were protagonists of the theological conflicts of the 4th and 5th centuries, but it is also the city where Christianity retained a number of privileges during the Seljuk period, and that it is also home to some of the most important monuments of Seljuk art. Moreover, the Teke - i.e. the community and mausoleum - of Mevlana Celaleddin Rumi, founder of the mystic order of the Whirling Dervishes, is also located in Inconium.

The Apostles, as was their usual custom, went to the synagogue of Inconium and found themselves among a large number of Jews and Greeks, as the Acts tell us (14:1ff). Many believed the enthusiastic words of Paul and Barnabas, who were full of the courage that their faith in Christ gave them. At some point, however, the same thing that had happened on their previous stops happened here too. The people were divided and those who were criticising them started to throw stones. For one more time, then, Paul and Barnabas were forced to abandon a city, having, however, managed to sow the seeds of the Word of God here before making their way to Lystra and Derbe.

While preaching at Lystra Paul began to cure a man who had been crippled from birth. What followed this miracle in indescribable. The crowd believed Paul and Barnabas to be Hermes and Zeus come to them in human form. The priest of Zeus even lead oxen to the front of the city and prepared to sacrifice them in their honour!

"*Men, why are you doing these things?*" the Apostles said tearing off their clothes. "*We also are men with the same nature as you, and preach to you that you should turn from these useless things to the living God*". With these words they were able to restrain the frenzy of the crowd. Yet some in the crowd had been egged on by the Jews who had arrived from Antioch and Inconium. They started stoning Paul and then dragged him out of the city, believing him to be dead. With the succour of the faithful he recovered and the next day left with Barnabas for Derbe. They later returned to Lystra, from there visiting Inconium and Antioch, constantly teaching and emboldening their disciples and ordaining priests at every church. They then crossed Pisidia and Pamphylia preaching, visited Perga again, finally reaching Attalia.

Attalia, a port in our day too, lying on the south coast of Asia Minor, was founded in the 2nd century BC by Attalos II Philadelphus, the King of Pergamon. Attalos has gone down in history for his love and devotion to his brother Eumenes II and as the founder of the Stoa which bears his name in the Ancient Agora of Athens. This Stoa has now been fully restored. Paul and Barnabas embarked upon their boat at Attalia and set sail for Antioch, from where they had started, in order to complete the work that had been assigned to them, and they remained here among other Christians for some time.

Bronze Age jar,
first half 5th millennium.

SECOND MISSION (AD 49-52)

At the Jerusalem Council, which took place some time between the First and the Second Missions, there was a great discussion as to whether circumcision be practised or not, as some were arguing. The Council finally decided to send a letter to those Gentiles from Antioch, Syria and Cilicia who had converted to Christianity. In the letter it was emphasised *"that you abstain from things offered to idols, from blood, from things strangled and from prostitution. If you keep yourselves from these you will do well"* (Acts 15:29). Paul and Barnabas, along with Silas and Barsabas took this message, with Paul and Barnabas staying for a period in Antioch teaching.

One day, when Paul and Barnabas were talking, Paul suggested that they go on a journey to all the places where they had preached to see how the Christians there were doing.

And then something happened that nobody could foresee. The two men had a disagreement that was so great and created such a deep division between them that they each chose their own separate road. The cause was Barnabas's insistence that they include John Mark in their entourage, who had previously abandoned them during the First Mission in Pamphylia. Paul refused to take him again, and Barnabas was so unyielding that he took John Mark with him and left for Cyprus. Paul chose Silas as his travel companion and they soon set off. The year must now be AD 49.

The two Apostles crossed Syria and Cilicia, passing through Derbe to reach Lystra. In this city their entourage was joined by Timothy, the son of a Greek man and a Jewish woman and a disciple who was especially respected by the people of the region. Wherever they passed they took the message of the Apostles and the Elders from Jerusalem, and, as the Acts (16:5) testify, the churches became stronger and with constantly increasing numbers. They continued on their road towards Phrygia and Galatia, going past Mysia and reaching Troas.

ON THE ROAD FOR TROAS

This region, the north-west section of Asia Minor, touches upon the shores of the Propontis, the Hellespont, the Aegean and the Adramytios Gulf, and was cut across by the Granikos, Skamander, Simoe, Aesop, Risos, Euneos and other rivers. Homer provides many details about this land, which was made legendary by the war which took place there, *"for an empty shirt, for a Helen"*. Many kingdoms had emerged in the area, coming under the general stewardship of Priam (Troy, Dardania, Abydos, Thebes, Pedasos, Lyrnissos). Homer eulogised the region and the heroic events connected to the siege of Troy. Many years later the burning desire and enthusiasm of Heinrich Schliemann turned the myth into history. His excavations, conducted between 1870 and 1890, led to the discovery of Troy and the hill of Hisarlik, between the Scamander and Simoen rivers, that had their estuaries at the mouth of the Hellespont. Schliemann's book on the excavation provides for a fascinating reading and description of the events that he lived there. Some years later Dörpfeld would confirm the identification of Schliemann's archaeological discovery with Homeric Troy, determining that Layers 6 and 7 (of a total nine successive layers) were contemporaneous with Mycenae and Tiryns.

Many years later, between 1932 and 1938, the Cincinnati archaeological mission, led by Carl Blegen, would determine conclusively that the remains from the seventh settlement at Troy provide evidence of destruction by fire. Since this layer dates to the mid-13th century BC, these remains must be considered to be the remains of Homeric Troy.

It was here in Troas, then, where Paul saw a vision in his sleep of a tall, striking Macedonian standing in front of him and pleading with him to *"Come over to Macedonia and help us"* (Acts 16:9). The author of the Acts records at this point: *"Now after he had seen the vision, immediately we sought to go to Macedonia, concluding that the Lord had called us to preach the gospel to them"* (Acts 16:10).

At this point it should be noted that it is known that the author of the Acts was the Evangelist Luke, a doctor from Antioch, a city which he often praises in his own way. He understood the historical methodology of his day and had had a Greek education. He wrote the third and most synoptic Gospel and is thought to have been the companion of Cleopas on the way to Emmaus.

Based on his texts, specialists believe that Luke joined up with Paul and Silas at Troas, and from this point on the so-called "we" verses can be observed, where the author writes in the first person.

The moment, then, at which their immediate departure was decided is of exceptional importance for Paul's journey. This is the point at which his great, unique, unsurpassed and redemptive relationship with the Greeks begins.

The walls of Troy.

SAMOTHRACE

The sanctuary of the Kabeiroi, Samothrace.

"herefore sailing from Troas, we ran a straight course to Samothrace, and the next day came to Neapolis" (Acts 16:11-12).

In the north-east Aegean, south of Alexandroupolis, lies Samothrace, the third largest island in the Aegean. Its tallest mountain is the Saos (1,664 m) and it is lush green, with plenty of therapeutic waters. With traces of habitation from the Late Neolithic period, it flourished in Hellenistic times (3rd-2nd century BC). The Romans considered it their first place of origin as it was home to Dardanos, ancestor of Aeneas.

Samothrace was famous throughout antiquity for the worship of the Kabeiroi, the Great Gods, divinities who were otherwise foreign to the ancient Greek pantheon. In contrast to that at Eleusis, the sanctuary at Samothrace was open to all the uninitiated, and people from all classes and lands could be initiated into the Mysteries of the Kabeiroi. It is typical that the life of Arsinoe was so closely connected both during her first and her second marriage to the sanctuary of the Kabeiroi. Its remains cover a wide area of around 50,000 square metres near the island's north-west coast.

The Tholos, or Rotunda, of Arsinoe II was built between 280 and 270 BC and is considered to have been the

1

2

largest circular building in the ancient Greek world. The remains of other buildings here include the Anaktoron, the Hall of Votive Gifts, the Altar Court and the Theatre. The building with the Dancers, known as the Temenos, is the site's largest and oldest marble building, constructed in around 340 BC, perhaps as a votive offering by Phillip. Work on the Hieron, a Doric building in which the *epoptia,* the highest level of initiation, were conducted started in 325 BC to be completed in around 150 BC. These buildings were the most important in the sanctuary of the Great Gods, and the visitor can today explore them in the archaeological site of Palaiopolis, the ancient city of Samothrace.

To the south of the theatre, of which there are few remains, is the Nike Monument in which the famous Winged Victory, or Nike of Samothrace, had stood. It was found in 1863 by the French Consul to the Sublime Porte Ch. Champoiseau and is now in the Louvre. A work of the Rhodian sculptor Pythokritos, it was made in 190-180 BC and is one of the most internationally renowned original works of Hellenistic art.

The Byzantines used Samothrace as a place of exile (Theophanes the Confessor, Constantine Lakapenos, etc.). It is recorded that in the 13th century its inhabitants took to piracy. They were conquered by the Turks, the Venetians and the Russians, and suffered complete destruction at the

hands of the Ottomans in 1821.

According to the traditions of the island, the Apostle Paul passed through Samothrace, anchoring at the port of the ancient city, today's Palaiopolis (the ancient mole is today sunken in the sea). An early Christian three-aisled basilica was later built on this site in remembrance of this event, using pieces from the architectural members of the ancient buildings in the construction. Inside the church are the scanty remains of a semi-circular apse and a section of the south wall of a second, single-aisled church which also used sections of ancient architectural members alongside the brickwork in its construction.

1. The Tholos of Arsinoe, or "Arsinoeion".
2. The ancient theatre.

The famous Nike of Samothrace, which today stands in the Louvre.

NEAPOLIS (KAVALA)

n the winter of AD 49 Paul disembarked for the first time on European soil after a journey with a fair wind lasting two days. This was at Neapolis, on the site where today's Kavala was later built. Around seven years later, when he was to find himself on the same spot for the second time, he would need five days (AD 56) to cover the same distance. Paul and his companions departed immediately for Philippi.

Neapolis, most likely a Thasian colony, was a fine port standing opposite Thasos, close to the delta of the River Nestos. It was founded in the mid-7th century BC, expanding into an important commercial centre. It was built on a point crossed by a very ancient road, which followed the natural lie of the land and led Thasos

to Macedonia and vice versa. A study of the historical sources shows that the Persians must have passed through here in 490 BC on their march towards southern Greece, and that Alexander the Great later set off for Asia from here.

The first inscribed silver coins from Neapolis date to 500 BC, with a gorgon on one side and a hollow square or swastika on the other. The minting of coins terminates in around 340 BC. In order to differentiate this Neapolis from the many others, coins minted here were inscribed with 'Neapolis in

Thrace' or 'Neapolis by Antisaran'.

Very little survives of the city's sanctuaries, public or private buildings. Some of the surviving evidence indicates that they worshipped the goddess Parthenos, a variation of the Thracian Artemis Tauropolos, also known as Bendis.

Neapolis is included in the tax catalogues of Athens from 454-453 BC, to which city she was always allied. Fragments from two honorary decrees relating to Neapolis have been found on the Acropolis at Athens. Once Phillip II had secured control of the area in 340 BC, Neapolis lost its autonomy and references to the city are rare. The city's name has been found on a milestone dating to the reign of Trajan (AD 106-107). This milestone records repair work done on the Via Egnatia along the route from Dyrrachium to Neapolis. Another milestone from the Via Egnatia dating to the late 2nd century AD has been discovered in Neapolis itself. There are very few early Christian remains left in the city. Fragments from early Christian breastplates, colonettes and columns have been brought to light in the vicinity of the church of Agios Nikolaos, where tradition holds that the Apostle Paul and his escort disembarked, as well as in the church of the Panagia, the Virgin. These remains provide evidence for the construction of monuments that have since been lost. The city still maintained its strategic importance during the reign of Justinian, and Heracles includes it among the 32 cities of Illyria in his Synekdemo.

The modern town of Kavala today stands on the site of ancient Neapolis, although from the ninth century AD onwards we find it referred to in the literary sources as Christoupolis. During the 14th century the Emperor Andronikos II Palaiologos built a small wall starting from Christoupolis and reaching as far as the peak of the mountain, thus cutting across the road, in order to prevent the approach of the Catalans. This wall, a section of which survives in the north part of Kavala, played an important defence role and during those years it appears that the site was occupied by a military base rather than a proper settlement. The city's third name, Kavala, probably first appears in the mid-15th century.

The city was rebuilt by Suleyman the Magnificent in around 1530. A new wall and aqueduct, which is preserved in excellent condition and is known as the Kamares, were built. The mosque of Imbraim Pasha Dzamisi must have been built around this time, and was later converted into today's church of Agios Nikolaos in the town centre. The area in front of the church has undergone redevelopment in the past few years, on the initiative of the Municipality and with the contribution of the well-known painter E. Varlamis. This artist has produced a canvas oil painting with a reconstruction of the moment when the Apostle Paul disembarked for the first time on European soil. Remains from the early Christian monuments

have been incorporated into the re-development of the site.

It should also be noted that Mehmet Ali, founder of the last Egyptian dynasty and father of Ibrahim, leader of the Ottoman forces in the Peloponnese during the Greek War of Independence, was born here in Kavala in 1769. He financed the building of a medrese, a college for Islamic instruction, in the city. This was the Imaret, which also had a poorhouse attached, and which still stands today.

The Apostle Paul landed in the vicinity of Agios Nikolaos and set off straight away along the Via Egnatia for Philippi, *"which is the foremost city of that part of Macedonia, a colony"* (Acts 16:12), located 22 kilometres from Neapolis. He was accompanied by Silas, Timothy and Luke.

The Via Egnatia was the large military road that connected Dyrrachium on the Adriatic coast with Byzantium, and which was built between 146 and 120 BC. It took its name from its builder, the proconsul Gaius Egnatius and was a decisive factor in the growth of the cities that lay along its route. Sections of the road have been found in Kavala a little before and a little after the Monastery of Agios Silas. It has recently been reconstructed along the route running from the Egnatia Hotel as far as the hill of the Monastery, and makes an excellent place for a walk.

1. The Ottoman building of the Imaret.
2. The old aqueduct, known as the Kamares.

PHILIPPI

nly a few Jews lived in Philippi, and for this reason it lacked a synagogue. On the Sabbath these few Jewish inhabitants would gather on the bank of a branch of the River Strymon, in an evocative landscape. On the Sabbath that Paul went there for the first time only women had gathered. These women were the first people in the whole of Europe to hear the teachings of Saint Paul. Among them was Lydia, a pious woman from Thyatira in Asia Minor. She sold purple from Phrygia, shells from which they would remove the dye in order to colour luxury materials. She was the first person to be baptised a Christian in Europe and helped greatly to spread the Word of the Lord.

As Paul and his escort made their way to the place of worship they met a young slave girl who was possessed with the 'spirit of the Python', i.e. the power of divination, which brought great profit for her masters. Python, along with Gaia, were demonic powers - personifications of natural forces - who were the guardians of the Oracle at Delphi prior to Apollo. *"These men are the servants of the Most High God, who proclaim to us the way of salvation"*, she cried out and followed the Apostle and his escort, repeating the same words for several days. At some point Paul became annoyed and, turning to the girl, said to the spirit *"I command you in the name of Jesus Christ to come out of her"*. The child was immediately freed from the 'sprit of the Python'. Her masters, however, seeing that their profit from this activity was lost, accused Paul and Silas of bringing trouble to the city and of teaching customs that were not lawful for them as Romans. The two men were beaten with rods and thrown bound into prison. Yet they did not lose their faith and prayed and sang hymns in front of all the prisoners. But at midnight there was a great earthquake that caused much panic. The doors of the prison opened and the prison guard, believing that all the prisoners had escaped, attempted to kill himself. The two Apostles stopped him, however, and he started to believe in God. The guard hosted them in his house and washed their wounds, and they baptised him and his whole family. The next day the magistrates, shocked by the events of the night before, were informed that they had imprisoned Roman citizens. Frightened, they apologised to them and requested them, from fear of further trouble, to leave the city. Paul refused however, saying *"They have beaten us openly, uncondemned Romans, and have thrown us into prison. And now they put us out secretly? No indeed. Let*

he church of Saint Lydia.

The baptistry of Saint Lydia.

them come themselves and get us out". The officers were forced to acquiesce, and they went and set them free.

The Apostles went to Lydia's house, where they were accommodated. They saw the faithful, gave them encouragement, and departed for Thessaloniki once they had bid them goodbye. Paul was to maintain close ties with the Philippians, who supported him financially on many occasions, even when he found himself imprisoned in Rome. He sent them an Epistle from there, in which he exhorted: *"Do all things without complaining and disputing, that you may become blameless and harmless, children of God without fault in the midst of a crooked and perverse generation, among whom you shine as lights in the world, holding fast the word of life"* (Phil. 2:14-16). Seven years after his first visit, in the autumn of 56, he was to find himself in Phillipi again, and was to make another three journeys there, in April 57, the spring of 63 and the winter of 64.

There is evidence of human settlement in the vicinity of the site where Phillipi was later to be built 5,000 years before the Birth of Christ. The prehistoric settlement of Dikili Tach was discovered near here. Centuries later, in 360 BC, Thasians, led by the Athenian Kallistratos, were to found a colony a short distance from here. They called it Krenides ('Fountains') because it had many springs. Two large rivers, the Strymon and the Nestos,

irrigate its soil. Close to the verdant Mount Pangaios, rich in metals, and on the foothills of Mount Orbelos, the colonists struggled to build their settlement, under the constant pressure of the local Thracian tribes. They fled to Philippi, which was on an excellent site, both in terms of wealth and as a communications hub. Colonists settled here, fortifying the site and later naming it Philppi (356 BC). In 168 BC it was taken by the Romans. The Battle of Phillipi took place in 42 BC, in which the Roman troops of Antony and Octavian fought with those of Brutus and Cassisus. The republicans, i.e. Brutus and Cassius, were defeated and Roman colonists and veteran soldiers then settled here. The city was renamed Colonia Augusta Julia Philippensis – i.e. it became a Roman colony - and its inhabitants acquired the rights of Roman citizens.

The population increased and the economy flourished. The population was very diverse, and these various elements had a significant influence on local society, with a variety of religions (Thracian, Greek, Eastern). The city's strict adherence to Roman laws, as seen in the example of the treatment of Paul, is revealing as is the economic ease and fraternal spirit evidenced in the financial support given to Paul. As he noted in his epistle to the Philippians: *"In the beginning of the gospel, when I departed from Macedonia, no church shared with me concerning giving and receiving but you only"* (Phil. 4:15).

The early Christian Basilica B at Philippi (6th century).

1. *Detail from the early Christian Basilica B.*
2. *The Forum and ruins of the early Christian octagonal building.*
3. *The early Christian Basilica A.*

The large archaeological site, and the early Christian basilicas in particular, are testimony to the importance of the city of Phillipi. The Via Egnatia divided the city in two, and sections of it have been found on the north side of the Forum of Phillipi and near today's Baptistery, on the branch of the River Strymon.

The Forum, built along a unified plan in 150 BC with stoas, shops (amongst them is one that was said to have been Lydia's), a palaestra and baths, was discovered in the section of the city to the south of the Via Egnatia. The Forum is a giant square that was surrounded by many buildings, the dimensions of which reach 178 x 70 m. Basilica B was built on top of the palaestra, on the south side of the Forum, in the 6th century.

Built at the most central point of Philippi around AD 550, this was a domed basilica, some points of which survive to a significant height, and it was decorated with column capitals, cornices and pillars with carved decoration produced with a drill and of excellent craftsmanship. After its destruction, in the mid-6th century, the narthex, which was still standing, was converted into a small church. The Octagon, an early Christian church dedicated to the Apostle Paul, the Metropolitan church of Phillipi (5th century), was discovered on the east side of the Forum.

Mosaic floor from the house of worship dedicated to St Paul.

It was surrounded by baths, hostels, the Bishop's residence and store rooms. It is worth noting that the site of the Octagon had previously been occupied by a Hellenistic burial, which in AD 313 under Bishop Porphyrus was converted into a chapel with mosaics. It is the earliest place of worship dedicated to the Apostle Paul, as we can see from a surviving inscription: "Porphyrus the Bishop made the adornment of the Basilica of Paul in Christ". To the north of the section of the city with the Via Egnatia is Basilica A, the largest early Christian church in Phillipi (late 5th century). After this building was destroyed (perhaps in around 600), worship was limited to a small church with a subterranean crypt in its southwest corner. Tradition holds that this

was the prison of St Paul. This building had perhaps originally been a Roman well which the Christians converted into a baptistery and later into a chapel, to which they added some fine wall paintings. A little to the west there is another basilica, Basilica C, which also lies to the east of the 4th-century theatre. In around AD 20-30 this theatre was converted into an arena and, despite the successive alterations that were made to it, it survives in quite good condition at some points.

On the Acropolis are the remains of mid- and late-Byzantine towers, at its foot are the remains of a temple to Roman divinities, whilst outside the walls there are Roman and early Christian cemeteries, including churchyards. Tradition holds that the burial

The ancient theatre.

monument (a stone sarcophagus) of the veteran C. Vidius Quartus was the 'manger of Bucephalus'. The Romans called old soldiers of every rank who had completed their military duties, which lasted for 16–26 years, Veterani. Bucephalus was also the name of Alexander the Great's famous horse. This was the Macedonian king's beloved horse and he had managed to tame it in a very subtle way, by turning its head to the sun so that it would not see its shadow, which frightened and agitated it. The animal died at the age of 30 years after the battle on the River Hydaspes, and Alexander named one of the many cities that he founded after his horse.

In the past few years an impressive octagonal church and Baptistery has been built on the point where Saint Paul

taught. It is adorned with the wonderful mosaics of Vlassis Tsotsonis and the glass tablets of Meropi Preka, and bears an undeniable testimony to the age-old bond between the city of Phillipi and its Teacher and spiritual Father.

Underground crypt, which is considered to be Saint Paul's prison.

AMPHIPOLIS

The Lion of Amphipolis.

aint Paul and his escort left Phillipi along the Via Egnatia and went quickly in the direction of Thessaloniki. In the

Amphipolis was one of the most important cities of Macedonia. It was founded in 437/6 BC by the general

it during the Peloponnesian War in 422 BC, an event eloquently described by Thucydides. During this celebrated battle both Brasidas the leader of the victors and Kleon leader of the Athenians were killed. Mention must be made of its careful fortifications, the earlier phase of which dates to the classical period and the later to the Hellenistic period, with their five towers. A length of 207 m has survived in the north section of the wall, the height of which reaches around 7 m. The most important of the towers was the so-called Tower C in the north-west of the city. The road that passed over the bridge on the river Strymon, which Thucydides mentions when discussing the events of 422 BC (4.103 ff.) led up to this tower. It is quite amazing that today's visitor can see a fairly extensive part of the tower, including round and square posts from the classical, Roman and Byzantine years, as well as nails and some planks.

A symbol of Amphipolis is the Lion, a tomb monument of the 4th century BC that is attributed to the admiral Laomedon. Amphipolis prospered greatly during the reign of Phillip II, and three of Alexander's most distinguished admirals, Nearchus, Androsthenis and Laomedon were sons of the city. During the Roman period it was the administrative seat of one of the four regions into which the Romans had divided Macedonia, the First Region or Makedonia Proti.

This is where Alexander the Great embarked upon his campaign and

where Roxane and her son were killed. This is where Zoilos the Homeromastix ('scourge of Homer'), a 4th-century sophist, and Pamphilus, tutor of Apelles and Pausias, were born.

The city's impressive prosperity during the Roman period can be seen in the fact that the Via Egnatia passed through here. The monuments dating to the Roman period are not, however, so impressive. During the early Christian period the city was the seat of a Bishopric and an important religious centre, as can be seen from the discovery by archaeologists of Christian basilicas and sections of an early Christian church. It is believed that Amphipolis was destroyed sometime in the 8th-9th century, to be re-inhabited in the 13th-14th century. The remains of two towers date to this period, one on each of the banks of the Strymon. The towers belong to Mount Athos and were perhaps used for storage, although at the same time they played the role of lookout posts for the passage into the hinterland.

The most impressive of the early Christian monuments of Amphipolis was discovered to the south of Basilica D. This was a 6th century central plan church, one of the very few examples of such a design in Greece. The core of it is a hexagon, although not so strictly laid out, that is enclosed by a wall and with a large atrium on the west side. The floors of the building were laid with marble tiles and marble mosaics of excellent craftsmanship.

APOLLONIA

pollonia was an ancient city of Mygdaonia in Macedonia, built on the south bank of Lake Volvi in 432 BC by Halkidians. The region was deemed particularly important for its strategic position throughout the Roman, Byzantine and Ottoman periods. Near the north side of the majestic temple of Apollo stood the Bema, or rostrum of Saint Paul. The waters of a spring that ran a little further down were considered to have been made holy by him.

In the early 20th century Apollonia was known as Pazarouda. Every week a grand bazaar was held here, mainly by Turks who had great respect for the miraculous powers of the water, believing that it could repel evil. At the same time, however, they would exploit it by taking money from the faithful who would came here to worship and receive the holy water.

Archaeological excavations have revealed a branch of the Via Egnatia that passed along the north side of the Volvi river, as well as the remains of Baths, a section of a defence wall and an old caravanserai, i.e. a hostel, which had been converted into simple agricultural buildings.

ACANTHUS

his city is not mentioned at all in the Acts of the Apostles. There is, however, a very old tradition that is strongly believed in the region according to which Saint Paul passed through here. Acanthus was an ancient colony of Andros, built on the prevailing religious ideas and had him imprisoned so that he would be tried and executed by the profligate Acanthians in a small cave near to today's site of Ierissos. Ierissos had been built on the site of ancient Acanthus but its position was

THESSALONIKI

 aint Paul arrived in Thessaloniki in the late autumn of AD 49. With him were Silas and Timothy, who, even though the author of the Acts does not name him is considered by specialists to have been well known to the Thessalonikans.

The city was completely different from those he had been in so far. Thessaloniki was a free city *(librae conditionis)* that had been under Roman rule since 168 BC, when it had been taken by the Roman consul Aemilius Paullus with the crushing defeat of Perseus at Pydna, the seat of a proconsul. Its population reached 220,000 residents.

It was founded in 315 BC by Cassander, who named the city after his wife, Thessaloniki, the sister of Alexander the Great. The city's location was not chosen by chance. Indeed, there were scattered Neolithic settlements in the rich plain through which large rivers flowed 2,500 years before the city was founded. One of these settlements Thermi, pre-existed on the site on which Thessaloniki was built, at the cove of the gulf mentioned by Herodotus a having been used by Xerxes as a naval and military base during his campaign against Greece. It had previously been believed that the Thermi on which Thessaloniki had either been built on or near was to be found near the medicinal springs at Sedes. More recent studies now place Thermi in the vicinity of Ano Toumba.

The city stretched out from the sea to the acropolis, forming a giant square within the walls, the oldest sections of which date to the Hellenistic period. It was cut across from east to west by the Via Regia of the Romans, known as the Leoforos or Avenue during the Byzantine period, on the site of today's Via Egnatia. This terminates to the west of the impressive Golden Gate, also known as the Vardar or Axios Gate. A fertile plain spreads out beyond the walls, with olive and vine groves and various other cultivations. The site was a key crossing point of the roads of the Balkans and the maritime routes leading from all the ports of the Mediterranean from a very early date, although not earlier than the era of Constantine the Great. Phillip V granted the city the right to mint bronze coins in the early 2nd century BC, and it subsequently shared in the same fate as the other cities of northern Greece when it was subjected to the Romans and later made capital of the Second Region of Macedonia.

The monuments with the squares, stoas, the annexes and the Odeion, the palace complex of Galerius Maximinian, the baths, the Hippodrome, the churches and all the other buildings and moveable finds that archaeological excavations have brought to the surface, such as the exceptionally fine mosaics, all bear witness to the wealth and cultural development of the Inhabitants.

The White Tower of Thessalonike.

The city of Thessaloniki.

In addition to the worship of the ancient Greek Pantheon, a particular flourishing of eastern religions can be witnessed throughout the Hellenistic and especially the Roman period, not to mention the emperor cults, Celtic deities and the Kabeiroi.

Inscriptions confirm the existence of a Hellenistic Agora, which it is believed lay in the vicinity of the later Roman Forum (Forum Romanum). The remains of a church dedicated to Serapis, which had already been consecrated in the 3rd century BC, have been found to the south-west of the Agora. The Forum Romanum extended on two levels from the Via Egnatia to Odos Olympou on two levels, thanks to the lay of the land. The Forum was formed by two parallel squares, bordered by stoas and the Odeion.

In the south square, known as the Megalophoros, is the famous Stoa of the Idols. This was a two-storey stoa with rich adornment, and some of its statues have been removed to the Louvre. The Forum dates to the late 2nd-early 3rd century AD, and the Odeion to AD 293-305.

Many Jews lived in Thessaloniki in the late 1st century BC, with a degree of wealth that afforded then a significant economic status. As we learn from the Acts, there was a synagogue in the city, close to the harbour, to which Paul went on three successive Sabbaths. The Acts of the Apostles (17:2 ff.) also narrate that he discussed with the people there, gave an interpretation of extracts from the Holy Scriptures that mention that Christ must be crucified and resurrected from the dead. *"This Jesus whom I preach*

The ancient Agora in the centre of the city.

to you is the Christ", he would tell them passionately. Some believed, and became disciples of Paul and Silas. Many Greeks were converted, including several women prominent in Thessaloniki society. How many were these first Christians is not known. It is, however, known that a Church was founded here.

Just as in Phillipi, problems soon arose in Thessaloniki and there were disturbances as a result of Paul's activities. How long the Apostles managed to stay in Thessaloniki is not known. The phrase *"for three Sabbaths "* (Acts 17:2) is considered by specialists to mean a period of four weeks.

Irrespective of this, the Jews of Thessaloniki used some shady characters from the market to rouse the rabble. Some went to the house of the newly baptised Jason, convinced that they would find Paul and his companions, who had managed to hide themselves, here. Jason and some other Christians were forcefully dragged to the politarchas, the rulers of the city, an institution that had been preserved from Hellenic Macedonian days. *"These who have turned the world upside down have come here too"*, they bellowed. *"Jason has harboured them, and these are all acting contrary to the decrees of Caesar, saying there is another king - Jesus"*. Jason and the others paid a monetary security and were set free, but that night Paul and his escort left Thessaloniki, where disturbances had already broken out. Tradition holds that he left quickly, hounded by his fellow Jews, and climbed out of the city walls at a high point, somewhere near where the Monastery of Vlatadon was later

built, perhaps through a small door. There was a stream a little to the east of the site of this Monastery. They say that Paul paused here briefly in order to refresh himself. The spring became known as "Saint Paul's holy water" and the Apostle's feast day was held here every year. After Greece annexed Thessaloniki, a church was built in the Saint's memory and the holy water was given a prominent place. In our day, a grand modern church stands to honour Saint Paul's visit to Thessaloniki and as an attestation of the fruits which grew from the seeds that he lay.

Paul never forgot the Christians he left behind Thessaloniki. The two letters to the Thessalonians are proof of this, bearing witness to his enduring interest in their spiritual and social progress, and in which he encourages, counsels and thanks them. This can also be seen in the fact that he sent Timothy to Thessaloniki to inform him of what was happening there. Both letters were written in Corinth. 1 Thessalians is believed to have been written in AD 51–52 and 2 Thessalians perhaps at the beginning of 53. It should be noted that the second Epistle was written by Paul, Silvanus and Timothy.

In the First Epistle to the Thessalians, he exhorts them to abstain from sexual immorality: *"For this is the will of God, your sanctification: that you should abstain from sexual immorality; that each of you should know how to possess his own vessel in sanctification and honour, not in passion of lust, like the Gentiles who do not know God"* (1 Thess. 4:3-5). He also makes mention of the Second Coming, with those famous words: *"But*

I do not want you to be ignorant, brethren, concerning those who have fallen asleep, lest you sorrow as others who have no hope..." And a little later he emphasises that "God did not appoint us to wrath, but to obtain salvation through our Lord Jesus Christ". At another point (1:6–8) he notes: *"so you became examples to all in Macedonia and Achaia who believe. For from you the word of the Lord has sounded forth, not only in Macedonia and Achaia, but also in every place. Your faith towards God has gone out, so that we do not need to say anything".*

The second Epistle is an attempt to clarify some of the issues relating to the Second Coming. Paul's teachings had stirred up such enthusiasm in Thessaloniki, that it led some to believe that the Second Coming would take place at any moment, with the result that they left their jobs and simply waited for the Second Coming without working. This letter has given us the famous maxims *"If anyone shall not work, neither shall he eat"* and *"stand fast and hold the traditions which you were taught, whether by word or our epistle".*

When Paul departed so quickly from Thessaloniki, he did so believing that he would return very soon. Seven whole years were to pass, and then again he hid in one house after another. Paul met two wonderful associates in Thessaloniki: Secundus, who accompanied him on his final mission and Aristarchus, who was jailed alongside him.

The growth of the city after the triumph of Christianity proves how right Paul was to favour it so much, and to praise it unreservedly for the faith, patience, stability and love of its people.

His arrival in Thessaloniki marks the beginning of a new chapter in the city's history. The Emperors of the later Roman Empire displayed a particular interest in Thessaloniki, valuing the city's fine strategic position, which helped it to survive as an important megalopolis until the beginning of the 4th century. After it had been raised to the status of capital of the part of the Empire that he had been granted (under the Tetrarchy), Galerius built a separate palace complex in the early 4th century, a substantial section of which survives today.

The south-east section of the Palace survives along Navarinou Square, with mosaics in some places. The Octagon, a particularly fine building, with the remains of marble mosaic flooring, has been discovered in the south-west of the Square. The architectural design of this building is reminiscent of the Mausoleum of Diocletian in Spalato, today's Dalmatian Split. Very few remains have survived until our period of the city's Hippodrome, which was located on the east side of town.

The Rotunda is a building of unknown purpose that was built in the early 4th century. Under Theodosius the Great it was converted into a church and in certain periods even served as the Metropolitan Church. Marble tiles that have not survived and some fine mosaics adorned the monument. When precisely they were produced is not known, but they are considered among the oldest surviving mosaics and perhaps date to the period when the monument was converted into a Christian church. The Rotunda was also later converted into a mosque. To this complex also belongs

the Kamara, otherwise known as the Arch of Galerius, a triumphant arch constructed in 305 to commemorate Galerius's definitive victory over the Persians and his military successes in the eastern provinces of the Roman empire. It is a particularly impressive example of its type.

Thessaoloniki emerged as a centre of worship of Saint Demetrius, the city's patron saint and guardian. The splendid basilica that was built on the remains of the Roman Bath in which Saint Demetrius had been imprisoned martyred and buried in 303 can be seen to the north of the Roman Forum. Marble tiles, mosaics, wall paintings, sculptures, column capitals, cornices, etc. of differing periods compose this unique monument. Originally built

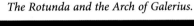

The Rotunda and the Arch of Galerius.

in 412-3 by the prefect Leontius, it was burnt down in 1917 and was reconsecrated in 1948. Beneath the crypt lies the place of the Saint's Martyrion, where he was martyred.

The Acheiropoietos, a double-aisled basilica with a wooden roof, was built in the mid-5th century. It is one of the rare examples of this type that have been preserved in such good condition, and was the first church that the Ottoman Emperor Murat occupied after the fall of Thessaloniki in 1430. It was reconsecrated in 1930.

Osios David is a little church dedicated to Christ the Saviour but received the name that it bears today out of some confusion that arose in the early 20th century. It was the cathedral church of the Monastery of Latomos and was built over an earlier Roman building in the late 5th-early 6th century.

Above: external view of Ayios Demetrios.

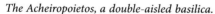

The Acheiropoietos, a double-aisled basilica.

The mosaic, unique for its subject matter, in the quarter-cycles of the apse, with a splendid representation of the vision of Ezekiel, also dates to this period.

Ayia Sophia, located at a central point of the city, was built in the mid-7th century over the ruins of an early Christian church that was three times the length. The characteristics of early Byzantine architecture were first introduced to the city with this monument. Historical and archaeological evidence confirms that in the narthex and the south section of the stoa area of Ayia Sophia were buried Bishops of Thessaloniki, such as Gregory Koutalis.

In 1028 Christophoros, a Byzantine official known as the *protospatharios*, built the church of the Panayia ton Chalkeon to the south-west of the ancient Agora. This is a cruciform, domed church built in brick, giving it a notable red colour.

The certain date of its construction provides us with a point of comparison for the dating of other monuments.

The church of Ayios Pandeleimon is a cross-in-square church near the Rotunda of Galerius, the cathedral church of an old monastery that was built in the late 13th-early 14th century, being converted into a mosque *ca* 1570.

Scholars believe that the church of Ayios Nikolaos Orphanos, once the cathedral of a Monastery located in the upper city, was built with proceeds from the Serbian krali (king) Milutin. The wall paintings date to 1310–1320 and belong to the Macedonian School of painting, although the name of the icon painter is not known. Some argue that he was G. Kalliergis whilst others

Interior of Ayios Demetrios.

The Panayia ton Chalkeon.

believe he was M. Astrapas or Eutychios. Ayios Efthymios is a chapel of Ayios Demetrius and was built as a double-aisled basilica to the north of the Roman Forum with proceeds from Michael Glavas Tarchaniotis, the *protostrator* or general commander. The wall paintings were done in 1303. Scholars believe that the wall paintings, which belong to the Macedonian School, may have been works of Panselinos, Astrapos or Euytchios. The church of Ayia Aikaterini in the north-west of the city, near the walls, also bears wall paintings of the Macedonian School. A complex cross-in-square church, it dates to 1320–1330 and its wall paintings have many similarities with those of the church of Ayios Nikolaos Orphanos.

The church of the Profitis Ilias is a marvellous example of ecclesiastical architecture of the Palaiologan period. This was the cathedral church of a 14th-century monastery, a particularly complex structure with features from Mount Athos. A few wall paintings remain, some of which date to the decade 1360-1370.

Saint Paul, Saint Peter and the Virgin with Child, wall painting from the church of Ayios Nikolaos Orphanos.

Section of the Eptapyrgion.

We mentioned above that the city's earliest defence walls were built during the Hellenistic period. Work began on a new wall in the mid-3rd century, although it was eventually completed in the 5th century. The first phase of construction appears rushed, as opposed to the later sections, which were carefully executed. A large part of their outer wall has been lost. Small inscriptions with monograms have been found at various points in the wall, which have helped in the dating of various of its sections.

The Acropolis and the building work that took place upon it are connected with the 5th century. On the north-east edge is the Eptapyrgion, composed of ten triangular and square towers and half-towers. Its construction reflects various building phases, from the early Byzantine to the Ottoman period, thus making it difficult to classify the building phases. It was used as a prison from the last decade of the 19th century, becoming known as the Yedi Koule. In 1989 it was evacuated and handed over to the Ministry of Culture as an archaeological monument.

In the past few years many burials from the early Christian centuries have come to light in Thessaloniki. These have interesting paintings representing allegorical scenes from the Old and New Testaments. A splendid example of such a monument was excavated in the Municipality of Ambelokipoi in 1994.

BEREA

fter he left secretly for Berea, Paul walked along the Via Egnatia for a while, taking a different road at Pella, that cut through a wooded, fertile and idyllic region.

Berea at that time was capital of the third administrative district of Macedonia (Third Region), with a substantial population. The city was pinned onto the foothills of lush Mount Vermio, rooted on the same soil since its foundation, an event that has been lost in the mist of time. The Macedonians settled here in around 700 BC, although the first historical reference is found in Thucydides, when he talks about the Athenian operations against Potidaia. Berea shared the fate of the other Macedonian cities and came under Roman rule in 168 BC, emerging as one of the most important cities of Macedonia during the Roman Empire. Sections of Roman roads that led in different directions have survived in the centre of Berea today. Other remains from the Roman period include the ruins of various private and public buildings, Baths, Hellenistic and Roman burials, etc. In 1204 the city came under Latin rule for a decade, passing to the Despotate of Epirus and then to the Empire of Nikaia. In 1387 the Ottomans took it, and it became a part of Greece in 1912 after the Balkan War. There was a flourishing Jewish synagogue here. As is written in the Acts, when Paul and Silas *"arrived, they went into the synagogue of the Jews"* (17: 10) indicating that the Apostles went straight to the synagogue on their arrival. It is also mentioned that the Jews of Berea were more courteous than those of Thessaloniki, and they listened to Saint Paul's teaching of the Gospel with great interest. Among the listeners were people who belonged to the wealthy classes, Jews and converts, and a large number of women.

The Apostle's enemies in Thessaloniki were informed of his activities in Berea, and sent men there to create a disturbance. Paul's companions immediately took him far away from Berea, although Timothy and Silas remained there. The new Church needed them. During Paul's sojourn in Berea the people were studying the Holy Scripture with great interest. Somebody had to stay, therefore. In any case, the wrath of the enemies was directed at Paul. As a gift Berea gave the Apostle to the Gentiles an associate, Sopater the son of Pyrrhus, who later accompanied him on his return through Asia.

*Traditional nooks
and a general view of Berea.*

The point at which Paul is believed to have stood and preached the Gospel in Berea, the so-called Bema of the Apostle Paul, has been dramatically adorned in our days. The Pauleia, a series of religious, cultural, athletic and artistic events, have been organised since 1995, rounded off each time with an academic conference.

The Apostolic Church of Berea has continued its redemptive work unceasingly since its foundation. A series of fifty churches, small and large, of various periods, provides undeniable proof of this mission and the living faith of the people of Berea. Among these stands out the small basilica church of the Resurrection of Christ. Paintings survive on its outer walls of the 'deceased' of the 14th and 18th century, whilst the inscriptions that survive on the monument provide much information about the church. Its founder was Xenos Psalidas and the monument was completed with the contribution of his wife Euphrosyne during the reign of the Emperor Andronikos Komnenos Palaiologos. What makes this monument unique are the wall paintings produced in 1315 by the great Thessalonikan icon painter Gregorios Kallergis, one of the leading representatives of the Macedonian School. The Monastery of Panayia Soumela has been founded

1. Monument near the Bema of the Apostle Paul.
2. Church in the centre of the town.
3, 5. The church of the Resurrection of Christ and wall paintings from its interior.
4. Priests at the Bema of the Apostle Paul.

near the village of Katania, at a short distance from Berea. This is where the miracle-working icon of the Panayia Soumela had been brought from the Black Sea Pontos region. This is the 'family' icon and shrine of all Pontians - Greeks descending from the Pontus region - throughout the world. The Monastery of the Timiou Prodromou Skitis of Berea is set in a magical spot above the River Aliakmona, in which Saint Grigorios Palamas, Archbishop of Thessaloniki and great teacher of mystic theology, served as a monk for five years. The neighbourhood around Berea, with the Palaces and the magnificent burials at Vergina, should not be overlooked.

1, 2, 3. The cathedral church of
   the Panayia Soumela.
4. The archaeological site of Vergina.
5. Ancient public baths at Dion.

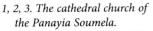

The Acropolis and the Odeion of Herodes Atticus.
The Lycabettus hill can be seen in the background.

ATHENS

n AD 51 Saint Paul travelled from Berea to Athens by boat. The journey overland then lasted for around twelve days. The Acts mention that his escort accompanied him as far as Athens and then returned with the order to tell Timothy and Silas that they should meet him at the earliest possible opportunity.

If we were to give even a brief description of Athens from the Neolithic period until the last few centuries, it would require far more space than is available in this book. If we were to limit ourselves to the last pre-Christian centuries, then mention must be made of the emergence of Macedonia as the leading power in Greece, putting Athens into decline from the mid-4th century and making her dependent upon Macedonian policy, particularly after the death of Alexander the Great. A brief period under the influence of Pergamon and Ptolemaic Egypt indicates that the flame of the brilliant past and its radiance had not completely died out, and the Roman administration privileged Athens over other parts of the Empire. It was certainly sacked by Sulla in 86 BC, but many leading Roman cultural and political figures, such as Cicero, Horace, Ovid, Propertius, Mark Antony and Brutus visited the city, drawn by its beauties and its education. The benefactions of Hadrian and Herodes Atticus were unsurpassed, and their rich contributions made the construction of a number of splendid public buildings possible. We shall therefore focus our attention on providing a synoptic picture of Athens in the centuries a little before and a little after the arrival of Saint Paul, and give an account of certain monuments.

Athens in the mid-first century AD was quite different from the brilliant city of the classical period. The works of art had been systematically plundered, the Roman conquest had made a wasteland of the city of Pallas Athena and the decline in moral values was palpable.

During the Imperial period, between 17 and 10 BC, a temple to Rome and Augustus was built on the Athens Acropolis to the east of the Parthenon, in an effort on the part of the Athenians to propitiate the Roman Emperor. The pedestal for the statue of Eumenes II, victor in the Panathenaic Games of 178 BC, was built in front of the Propylaia.

1. The Erectheion with the so-called Caryatids.
2. The temple of Hephaestus and the church of the Ayii Apostoli near the ancient Agora.

A revival of building activity in the Athens *Agora* can be witnessed during the 2nd century BC. The Middle and East Stoa, the East Building and a small annex of the Metroon, which replaced the Old Bouleuterion, were built. The remodelling of the Agora during the 2nd century constituted its basic form for almost the rest of the ancient period. In the 2nd century AD, the Library of Pantainos was built in the south-east corner of the Agora, the Odeion of Agrippa was renovated and the Library of Hadrian built to the east of the Stoa of Attalus. Only the Stoa of Attalus and the temple of Hephaestus survived the Herulian raid (AD 267), although, just like the Parthenon, the temple of Hephaestus was converted into a Christian church.

The Roman Forum lies to the east of the ancient Agora. In its vicinity, and in very good condition, survives the first-century BC water clock, the Horologion of Andronikos Kyrrestes also known as the Tower of the Winds or the Aeredes from the relief frieze with the personified winds. On its roof there was a weather vane, sundial and water clock. The Stoa

of Eumenes (196-159 BC) extends from the west of the Theatre of Dionysus as far as the Odeion of Herodes Atticus.

The Arch of Hadrian, built by the Athenians in the Emperor's honour, stands to the east of the Acropolis and divided the ancient city from that which spread during the Roman period. A little further along lies the temple of Olympian Zeus (or Olympeion), work on which started in the 6th century BC only to be completed in the 2nd century AD with funds provided by Hadrian, a few columns of which remain standing today.

1. The Stoa of Attalus.
2. The Roman Forum with the Horolgion of Andronikos Kyrrestes.
3. The Arch of Hadrian.
4. The columns of the temple of Olympian Zeus.

The ancient Odos Tripodon, or 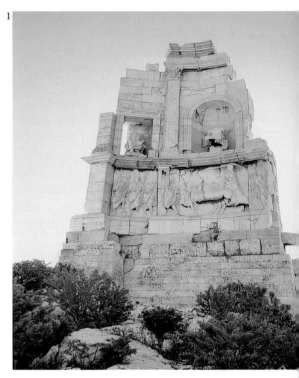 Tripodon Street, leading from the Agora to the temple of Dionysus and then further east, coincides with the modern street of the same name. Choregic monuments were set up along this street, upon which were placed the Tripods that were given as trophies in the dramatic contests, primarily during the 4th century. Among the better known, which survive in good condition today, is the choregic monument to Lysikrates (334 BC), which owes its good condition to the fact that it was incorporated into the building of the Capuchin Convent during the Ottoman period. The Stadium was built on the foothills of the Ardettos hill in the 2nd century AD, from which point the city began to expand to the east, beyond the Themistoklean Wall. A wall was erected in the mid-3rd century, with material from the Olympeion being used in its construction.

The burial monument to C. Julius Antiochus Philoppapus on the Mouseion hill, also known as Philopappou hill, to the south of the Acropolis, was constructed in around AD 115. Philoppapus was the grandson of the last king of Commagene in northern Syria, who had settled in Athens and was a benefactor of the city. The closure of the philosophical schools under Justinian marks the beginning of the definitive decline of a city that is unique in world history for its art and culture.

1. Monument to the Muses
on Philoppapou hill.
2. The choregic monument of Lysikrates.

Many churches of the early Christian, Byzantine and post-Byzantine years survive around Athens. Next to today's metropolitan church is the church of the Panayia Gorgoepikoos (Ayios Eleftherios), built in the 11th century. Unique among its kind, it was completely built using marble from earlier buildings. The Sotiria Lykodemou is also known as the Russian Church because it was bought by the Russian community in 1852. An elegant church with characteristic decoration on its outer walls of a terracotta frieze with kufic script (first half of the 11th century). The Kapnikarea, a church built in the third quarter of the 11th century and dedicated to the Eisodia of the Virgin, with its repeated wall structures, the characteristic roof of the narthex and its idiosyncratic external form. To the 11th century also belongs the church of the SS Theodore in the south-west corner of the Kapnikarea. A little outside Athens, in the neighbourhood of Galatsi, is the Beautiful Church, also of the 11th century, dedicated to Saint George. The Daphne Monastery was built in the last third of the 11th century on the site of an ancient sanctuary of Apollo Daphneforos. Its architectural design is particularly elegant. The cathedral church is dedicated to the Dormition of the Virgin, with some splendid surviving mosaics. At the foot of Mount Hymettus is the Kaisariani Monastery, the cathedral church of which was built in the 11th century. Wall paintings of the 16th century survive. During the Ottoman period a series of scholars served as Abbot, and the Monastery had a fine library. This, however, was burnt down during the War of Independence, in which the Monastery played an active part.

The boat carrying the Apostle threw down its anchor at Faliro, the long-standing main port serving Athens. It was from here that Theseus left for Crete and Menestheus and his fifty ships for Troy. In the Ottoman period it was known as the Üç Burgaz, the 'three towers', which still stood up until the 19th century and which were used as prisons. The area of the harbour is defined as the expanse between the mouth of the Kifissos River until the little church of Agios Georgios. This is where the road from Athens which ended at the east Faliron Gate, the most important gate in the south side of the wall, started. This is the road that Saint Paul followed after he had disembarked from the boat. A century later the traveller Pausanias (1.1,4) was to observe that, *"The Athenians have another harbour at Mounychia with a temple of Mounychian Artemis, and one at Phaleron, as I said, with Demeter's sanctury beside it... and altars of the 'Unknown Gods'."*

In the Acts of the Apostles (17:23) Saint Paul does not describe exactly where he saw the altar of the 'Unknown Gods'. As he himself said, *"as I was passing through and considering"* - i.e. as I was passing and looking - *"I even found an altar with this inscription 'to the Unknown God'"*. It is very likely that he saw some of those altars mentioned by Pausanias. It should be noted that in the late antique period many people would dedicate altars and offerings to 'unknown gods', either from superstition, or because they wanted to pre-empt the consequences of neglecting gods that they were not aware of.

In the Acts of the Apostles, chapter 17 (16–34), an account is given of Paul's stay and activities in Athens. Whilst waiting for Silas and Timothy to come from Macedonia, he would stroll around the city and talk with the citizens in the synagogue and the *Agora,* and the plethora of idols and icons disturbed him. On the other hand, his teachings about the crucifixion, death and resurrection of Jesus fuelled some Epicurean and Stoic philosophers to call him a 'babbler'. Paul was not, however, persecuted in Athens for his teachings. On the contrary, he was invited to the Areopagus to present his teachings analytically since, as the Acts remark, *"For all the Athenians and all the foreigners who were there spent their time in nothing else but either to tell or hear something new"* (17:21).

The Areopagus was principally the hill to the west of the Acropolis. This is where, according to mythology, all those who had committed murder were tried. Archaeological evidence indicates the worship of the Semnai or Erinyes (the Furies), spirits, which sought blood vengeance. The area was associated from a very early date with the *ex Areiou Pagou Boule,* the Council of the Areopagus, the court which judged on cases of manslaughter in the Areopagus. For other cases, its members would meet at the seat of the Archon Basileus, one of the city's most important officials, in the Stoa Basileus in the Agora. This stoa

St Dionysios the Areopagite. Wall painting from the Sacred Bema of the Holy Monastery of Dionysios.

was one of the most celebrated public buildings in Athens, and its ruins first came to light in 1970 beneath the trench of the electric railway line. It was used as a kind of archive for the principal laws of the city, and after Solon's reforms became home to the Basileus and was also used for formal meals. The *Boule*, or Council, of the Areopagus is believed to have met in an open area in front of the Stoa as the space within is limited. Near the rock of the Areopagus are the remains of the Iobacheion, a meeting ground for worshippers of an eastern mystery religion, and the remains of the church of Saint Dionysios the Areopagite. This was built in the 7th or 8th century and renovated in the 11th century. Few traces of this church have survived on the north side of the Areopagus. Legend has it that Saint Paul hid within a spring near the site of the church in order to escape his idolatrous persecutors.

Paul's appearance in front of the Areopagus was certainly not insignificant. It has even been argued that the fact that one of the members of the court, Dionysios the Areopagite, embraced Christianity is directly related to this event.

Paul stood in the midst of the Areopagus, then, and said: *"Men of Athens, I perceive that in all things you are very religious; for as I was passing through and considering the objects of your worship, I even found an altar with the inscription: 'To the Unknown God'. Therefore, the One whom you worship without proclaiming knowing, I proclaim Him to you: God, who made the world and everything in it, since He is Lord of heaven and earth, does not dwell in temples made with hands. Nor is He worshipped with men's hands, as though He needed anything, since He gives to all life, breath and all things. And He has made from one blood every nation of men to dwell on all the face of the earth, and has determined their preappointed times and the boundaries of their dwellings, so that they might grope for Him and find Him, though He is not far from each one of us; for in Him we live and move and have our being, as also some of your own poets have said, 'For we are also His offspring'. Therefore, since we are the offspring of God, we ought not to think that the Divine Nature is like gold or silver or stone, something shaped by art and man's devising. Truly, these times of ignorance God overlooked, but now commands all men everywhere to repent, because He has appointed a day on which He will judge the world in righteousness by the Man whom He has ordained. He has given assurance of this to all by raising Him from the dead"*.

The Athenians listened to Paul with a repose that stemmed from their interest in new ideas and philosophical positions, something that was not hindered by the general climate of cultural and social decline that the Apostle witnessed in Athens. Yet, the issue of the raising of the dead was the point at which Paul's teaching of the Gospel in Athens could not go beyond. The immortality of the soul was, of course, one of the central points of Platonic teaching, but it was, however, very difficult for the teaching of the resurrection of the dead to find a willing audience in this city at this particular moment. Even so, his seminal

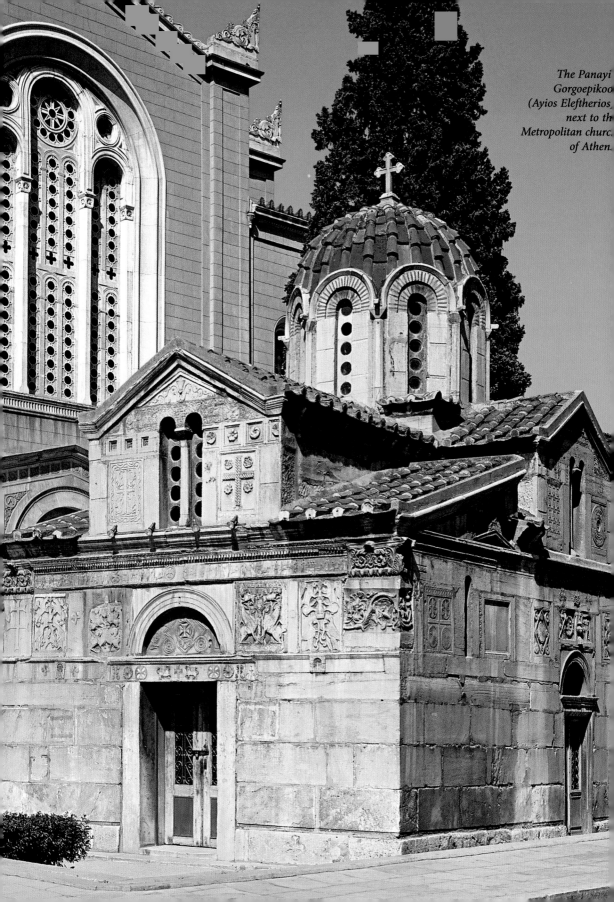

discourse was coming to the forefront. At the same time, the Greek aesthetic of beauty and nobility was a favourable factor in the spread of Paul's work, which taught the Athenians that: *"God, who made the world and everything in it, since He is Lord of heaven and earth, does not dwell in temples made with hands. Nor is He worshipped with men's hands, as though He needed anything, since He gives to all life, breath and all things"*.

Saint Dionysios the Areopagite is said to have travelled to Egypt during the time when Christ was crucified, to utter the famous phrase *"Either a God is suffering or the world is being destroyed"*, sensing on Good Friday how strange it was for it to go dark in the middle of the day. He and his whole family were baptised straight away as soon as he had heard Saint Paul. He was martyred most likely under Domitian, although other sources suggest this was during the reign of Trajan or Hadrian.

1. The Kapnikarea, dedicated to the Eisodia of the Virgin.
2. The Metropolitan church of Athens.

Christ Pantokrater, mosaic in the Daphne Monastery (11th century).

The patron saint of Athens and guardian of jurors, Saint Dionysios's feast day is held on 3 October, and, under a decision taken by the Church of Greece, he is claimed as a church founder. Others are also mentioned alongside him, such as Damaris.

A church dedicated to Saint Paul was built in 1887, close to the centre of Athens. Two years later Queen Olga, under the Bishop of Athens Procopius and with Lambros Kallifronas as Mayor, laid down the foundation stone of a newer, larger church designed by the architects Troubous and Schultz. In 1923 the Archbishop of Athens Chrysostomos Papadopoulos inaugurated the holding of Vespers on the feast day of Saint Paul on the Areopagus.

1, 2. Views of Kaisariani Monastery.
4. Daphne Monastery.

CORINTH

I t is not known which route Paul followed to reach Corinth. He may have gone overland and passed through Eleusis and Megara, yet he may also have gone by boat. What is certain is that he was troubled when he went, by the Athenians' reception of his teachings and by the situation of the churches in Macedonia. Already, whilst Paul was leaving Athens, Timothy was being expelled from Thessaloniki.

As a city, Corinth was completely different from that of Athens. Flourishing on trade with all the nations of the known world, it was full of people of every race and outlook whose presence created a new environment that was not at all reminiscent of the academic atmosphere of Athens. It was located at a key position for communications with the Peloponnese and the rest of Greece and was a bridge for journeys from the east to the west. The city's colonies formed a large chapter of the city's history: Syracuse, Corcyra, Croton, Ambracia, Sybari, Poseidonia, Lefkada, Anaktorio, Potidaia.

The archaic temple of Apollo at ancient Corinth.

The city was founded way back in the mist of time by Aletes, a descendant of Herakles, and it was governed by personages such as Kypselos and Periander. It stood by the side of Athens during the Peloponnesian War and for many years the activities of its governments were directly related to the fate of the other Greek cities during the classical and Hellenistic periods. In the Archaic period in particular there was a great economic and artistic activity, with brilliant pottery production, vase painting and bronze work. The Protocorinthian vases with the characteristic spherical aryballos design are particularly splendid. The city thus emerged as leader of the Achaian Confederacy, to be turned into a pile of rubble in 146 BC when it was subjugated to Rome by Mummius.

Around a hundred years passed, until the Romans decided to rebuild the city, founding a Roman colony on its ruins. Its population then comprised of both Greeks and Romans, freedmen and veterans, but also of people from all corners of the earth. Astarte and Melikertes, Kybele and Attis, Isis and Serapis, Dionysios and Poseidon, but especially Aphrodite Pandemos comprised a pantheon with a dark horizon, an antithesis to the charming natural environment that spread out around the city. New Corinth was built on the bedrock of the old, and new structures were added near to the destroyed older ones that were being renovated.

The Agora of Corinth is today a giant archaeological site. At its core was the magnificent, ancient Doric temple of Apollo, one of the most celebrated of antiquity. There were also many stoas and numerous shops, as well as smaller temples such as those dedicated to Tyche, Asklepios and Hermes. Also in the Agora was a sanctuary to Athena Halini, a theatre, Odeion, Baths and fountains, such as the Lerna, the Glauke and the Peirine, basilicas with sculptures of the imperial family, and large roads, such as the Lechaion Road. An unending complex of monuments, which Pausanias describes in great detail in his book on Corinth.

1. *The temple of Octavia.*
2. *The Roman Peirine fountain.*
3. *Corinthian capital.*
4. *The ancient Odeion.*

Towards the middle of the central row of shops was the Bema, the rostrum from which Roman officials addressed the citizens. In the Middle Ages a small temple was built on this spot, the foundations of which survive.

In the south-west of Corinth is the Acrocorinth, a conical hill that stands over the area, a fortress and hideout throughout all periods of history, very much associated with the life and death of Leo Sgouros.

Lechaion is the port of Corinth lying on the Corinthian Gulf. It is located closer to the city and in antiquity there were shipyards and a military naval station here. In Corinth's golden years long walls connected the port and naval station to the city, the remains of which were uncovered in the early 20th century. In the Roman period moles were built at Lechaion, which is located

on a very important strategic site, using very large porous stone blocks.

As part of the Roman renovation of Corinth, the city's second port was built at Kenchreai, on the Saronic Gulf close to the Isthmus. This port was well fortified and acted as a breakwater whenever there were great storms at sea. Most of the remains today lie under the sea and only a small section is on dry land. A small complex of rooms near to the south mole perhaps functioned as the port's warehouses. Next to them stood a small temple, perhaps dedicated to Isis, and the remains of a double-aisled basilica of the 4th century, beneath the floor of which were uncovered over seventy burials. Remains of late Roman and early Christian buildings lie near the north mole.

The castle of the Acrocorinth.

In the 1st century Kenchreai, which had been settled from the prehistoric period, had more inhabitants than Lechaion. This underlines Saint Paul's specific reference to the *"church in Kenchreai"* in his epistle to the Romans (16:1) and his introduction of the deacon Phoebe to the Romans, who delivered this epistle to Rome in the winter of 52-53. It was from the port of Kenchreai that Paul left for Ephesus with his escort in AD 53. It was at the point where the road from Kenchreai to the gate in the Corinth wall terminated that Alexander met the philosopher Diogenes whom, as is well known, lived in an earthenware pot.

The Acts of the Apostles mention (19:22) that Saint Paul sent his helpers Timothy and Erastus to Macedonia whilst he was in Ephesus. In his epistle to the Romans Paul refers to Erastus thus: *"Erastus the treasurer of the city, greets you"* (16:23). It appears that Erastus, who is counted among the Seventy Apostles, lived at the time that the epistle to the Romans was written in Corinth. An inscription has been found near the theatre of Corinth on which appears the name Erastus:

ERASTVS PRO AEDILITATE
S P STRAVIT

The inscription declares that the paving had been undertaken on the care of Erastus. The paving dates to the mid-1st century, but the inscription was carved later. It is believed that the Erastus of the inscription is one and the same as the treasurer of the city in

the time of Paul.

Sections of the Diolkos have been found in the vicinity of the Corinth Isthmus. This was a special kind of paved slipway upon which they would draw the boats from Kenchreai to Lechaion. It was constructed in the early 6th century BC under Periander and its purpose was to winch ships, particularly battle ships, speedily and in times of need. Many have tried to open a passage here, including Nero, yet without success. The canal was finally opened at the end of the 19th century and the opening ceremony took place on 28 October 1893, during the premiership of Harilaos Trikoupis.

Among the Christian monuments that suggest the magnitude of the Christian faith in Corinth is the giant early Christian basilica of Lechaion, the ruins of which were found near to the sea. Dedicated to Saint Leonidas, the total length of the monument from the nave to the edge of the outer atrium is 179 m!

In Corinth Paul came into contact with Aquila and Priscilla, who were also tentmakers and it appears that they were already aware of Jesus. Paul lived and worked with them, and taught to the Jews and the Greeks every Saturday. The majority of the Jews did not want to believe that Jesus was the Messiah and they condemned Paul. One day Paul shook the dust from his clothes and went to stay in the house of Titus Justus, who was a convert and lived near the synagogue.

Among those who believed was the ruler of the synagogue Crispus, who was baptised along with his family.

One night Paul heard the Lord say to him in a vision: *"Do not be afraid, but speak, and do not keep silent; for I am with you, and no one will attack you; for I have many people in this city"* (Acts 18:9-10). This is the first and only time when the Apostle would hear the voice of the Lord in Greece. In the meantime, Silas and Timothy had come from Macedonia and the number of those embracing Christianity was increasing. Some of these are among the best known names: Stephen, Fortunatus, Chloe and Achaikos. The newly baptised came from all the social classes, and it is calculated that Saint Paul went to Corinth at the beginning of AD 50 and remained there for a year and a half.

Section of the inscription with the name of Gallio found at Delphi.

The Acts of the Apostles tell us that the Jews of Corinth rose up against Paul, taking him to court on the charge that he was illegally attempting to persuade people to follow his teachings. At the Bema stood the proconsul Gallio, whose name has survived on an inscription at Delphi. This find has helped to provide a convincing chronology of this period of Paul's life. It should be noted that this Junius Gallio was the adoptive father of a brother of Seneca.

The actions of the Jews of Corinth did not have the results that they were seeking. Gallio heard them and, before Paul had a chance to open his mouth, said: *"If it were a matter of wrongdoing or wicked crimes there would be reason why I should bear with you. But if it is a question of words and names and your own law, look to it yourselves; for I do not want to be a judge of such matters"* (Acts 18:12-15). Gallio then had them removed, and paid no heed when the Greeks started to beat Sosthenes, the ruler of the synagogue, in front of the Bema. The Jews' charges against Paul to the proconsul bore no fruit, because Paul's problem was the enmity of his compatriots, not that of the idolaters. Despite the difficulties, the church of Corinth was growing.

Around eighteen months had passed when Saint Paul decided to leave Corinth, as he had to rush to Ephesus. He bid farewell to the brothers in the city and departed along with his escort of Silas, Timothy, Aquila and Priscilla.

In Ephesus he was to write his two 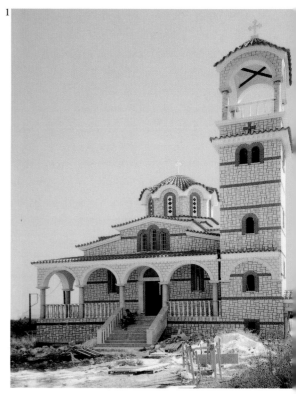 epistles to the Corinthians, in which he attempted to establish unity and eliminate differences. *"I plead with you, brethren, by the name of our Lord Jesus Christ, that you all speak the same thing, and that there be no divisions among you"* he wrote in 1 Corinthians (1:10). Later in the same epistle he wrote: *"For where there are envy, strife and divisions among you, are you not carnal and behaving like mere men?"* (3:3), and *"Therefore let no one boast in men. For all things are yours; whether Paul or Apollos or Cephas, or the world of life or death, or things present or things to come - all are yours. And you are Christ's, and Christ is God's"* (3:21-23).

He talks to the Corinthians about the power and strength of love, and

chapter 13 of 1 Corinthians is a 'Hymn to Love': *"Though I speak with the tongues of men and of angels, but have not love, I have become sounding brass or a clanging cymbal"* (13:1). In chapters 4-8, he writes: *"Love suffers long and is kind; love does not envy; love does not parade itself, is not puffed up; does not behave rudely, does not seek its own, thinks no evil; does not rejoice in iniquity, but rejoices in the truth; bears all things, believes all things, hopes all things, enjoys all things. Love never fails".*

Saint Paul is the patron saint of Corinth, and a splendid Cathedral Church was built in his honour. Recently another church, equally impressive and well cared for, was constructed very near the spot where he taught.

From Kenchreai Paul set off for Ephesus. A little before setting sail he cut his hair, to satisfy an old vow he had made. He stayed only a short while at Ephesus. With the promise to return soon, he embarked upon another ship and set sail for Antioch, stopping briefly at Caesarea in Palestine. It is said that he did not stay long at Antioch, and he was never to return there again. Silas was no longer following him, and quite why Paul was in such a hurry to get to Antioch or to Jerusalem or to both is not known.

1. *The church of St Paul near the Corinth archaeological site.*
2. *The metropolitan church of St Paul in the town of Corinth.*
3. *The Bema of St Paul in ancient Corinth.*

3

THIRD MISSION (AD 52 - 56)
EPHESUS

The third mission of Saint Paul began in AD 52 with his departure from Antioch. Crossing south Galatia and Phrygia with his disciples, he would counsel and support them. His destination was Ephesus, to fulfil the promise that he had given on his brief visit when returning from Corinth. In the three years that had passed, this city had become the base for his campaigns into Asia Minor, Greece and elsewhere.

Before following the Apostle on this journey, it is worth stopping for a little at Ephesus, this important city with its long history, the Ephesus of Revelations. The city which *"tested those who say they are apostles and are not, and have found them liars; and you have persevered and have patience, and [...] laboured and for My name's sake and have not become weary"* (Rev. 2: 2-3).

Ancient and Christian Ephesus covered an immense territory. From today's village of Selcuk (in memory of the Seljuk Turks who destroyed the city in 1116), where the church of Saint John the Evangelist and his grave lie, we proceed to the modern port of Kusadasi, passing the Aretemisium, the famous temple of Artemis and one of the Seven Wonders of the World. From here we enter the city in which Herakleios, Hipponax and Parasios were born, to admire the splendid monuments and lush green landscape, thanks to the waters of the Cayster River. The alluvial deposits from this river have transformed Ephesus from a coastal city to one that today lies eight kilometres from the sea.

The first builder of Ephesus was Androkles. In 541 BC the city was taken by Cyrus, and sided with the Persians during the Ionian Rebellion. During the Peloponnesian War it initially took the side of Athens, only to turn later to the Spartans. The firing of the Artemesium by Herostratos in 356 BC was a watershed. After the battle of Granikos, Alexander proposed to rebuild the temple, but only on the condition that his name be written on it. The answer, however, was that a 'god' cannot build a temple to another god.

A new era for the city started in 286 BC with Dysimachus, who took care to reorganise the building programme

The theatre of Ephesus,
with a seating capacity of 32,000.

1

for Ephesus's fortifications. At the beginning of the 1st century AD Augustus laid down a new town plan for Ephesus, now the capital of the province of Asia *(provincia Asia)*.

Ephesus grew into a heavily populated city, the second largest in size and population in the east after Alexandria and the third largest Christian city after Antioch and Jerusalem. The emperor Hadrian and his successors continued rebuilding and repairing its existing structures. The continuous inhabitation of the site for many centuries has meant that the buildings have been preserved with only the features of their last building phase. Mainly architectural remains and sculptural decoration survive from the archaic, classical and Hellenistic periods.

The remains of the famous temple of Artemis are so meagre as to be distressing. A single restored column is the main marker of the position of the monument, which was adorned with the works of the greatest artists of antiquity. Temples and sanctuaries of various gods, heroes and emperors, altars, marketplaces, Baths, Gymnasia and Stoas. A giant theatre with a capacity of 32,000, scene of the riots inspired by the silversmith Demetrius. The famous library known as the Library of Celsus, built in AD 117 by an heir of Tiberius Julius Celsus and which held at least 12,000 papyrus scrolls, a truly complex building with a war memorial and tomb.

2 Reconstruction work in recent years has restored to the Library facade the statues that, as inscriptions indicate, symbolised Eunoia (Goodwill), Arete (Excellence), Sophia (Wisdom) and Episteme (Knowledge). Aqueducts, Nymphaia, palaces and houses all lay witness to the extent, prosperity and importance of Ephesus. The Museum houses a large number of statues of Artemis Ephesia, depicting her in the characteristic manner with many breast-like nodes, symbolising fertility. On the lower part of her body there are many mythical and otherwise animals such as bulls, griffins and sphinxes, indicating her relationship with the animal kingdom.

3 Of the most important Christian monuments in Ephesus is the church of the Third Ecumenical Council, held in AD 431. This is a vast structure, the first church to be dedicated to the Virgin, built over an even larger building, with three successive reconstruction phases. The area around it is full of tombs. The existence of even a few ruined wall paintings in the church apse, stubbornly surviving the atmospheric conditions and anti-Christian ravages, is amazing.

1. The colossal statue of Ephesian Artemis, 2nd half of the 2nd century AD. Epehsus Museum.
2. The reconstructed column of the temple of Artemis.
3. The temple of Hadrian.

The Library of Celsus, built in AD 117.

The tomb of Saint John the Evangelist is to be found on the acropolis hill of the Byzantine period, otherwise known as Ayiasoluk, a corruption of Agios Theologos. The Saint died here in old age, after many years of teaching and writing. The ruins of the church of the Theologos in Ephesus are those of the basilica built by Justinian, and were discovered by G. Sotiriou in 1921-1922. The Asia Minor Disaster and the subsequent developments meant that the excavations have been continued by Austrian archaeologists since 1927.

The monument survives to a height of three metres at many points. The initial structure on this site consisted of a number of subterranean rooms, in which tradition places the tomb of Saint John. Later, in the 3rd or 4th century, a square mnemi, i.e. monument, was built on this spot. This formed the core of a cruciform basilica built by the Emperor Theodosius II (408-450), at which the Fathers of the Third Ecumenical Council worshipped. The church was built in the form of a Latin cross around this initial square building, which was comprised of four columns and a domed roof that covered the tomb. The east wing had five aisles, whilst the remainder were three aisled. In the following century, Justinian built a great new cruciform basilica, with narthex and atrium, on this spot, the total length of which reached 125 metres.

During his stay at Ephesus Paul would at first go to the synagogue and persuade the Jews with his teachings on Christ. When, however, some started to criticise him in front of the audience, he and his disciples moved to the school of an Ephesian named Tyrannus. He later also clashed with all those interested in the upkeep of the temple of Artemis, and in particular the preservation of her cult. Chapter 19 of the Acts of the Apostles discusses Paul's arrival here and the disturbances provoked by his work. There was a silversmith named Demetrius who manufactured silver shrines of Artemis, employing many craftsmen and with much work. One day Demetrius gathered his craftsmen and the other silversmiths in the theatre of the city and said to them: *"Men, you know that we have our prosperity by this trade. Moreover you see and hear that not only at Ephesus, but throughout almost all Asia, this Paul has persuaded and turned away many people, saying that they are not gods which are made with hands. So not only is this trade of ours in danger of falling into disrepute, but also the temple of the great goddess Artemis may be despised and her magnificence destroyed, whom all Asia and the world worship".*

His listeners became enraged and, faced with the prospect of unemployment, cried out *"Great is Artemis of the Ephesians"*. Crowds rushed into the theatre, seizing Paul's travelling companions Gaius and Aristarchus. Paul himself was held back by his disciples and did not appear at this gathering, even though he had expressed a desire to do so. The intervention of the more cool-headed city officials helped quell this dangerous disturbance, and calm was restored after some time.

1. View of the basilica of St John the Evangelist.
2. Central aisle of the cruciform basilica of St John the Evangelist. The Saint is buried at the spot with the four small columns in the centre.

IN GREECE ONCE MORE

Mansions in Mytilene town.

he details given in the Acts of the Apostles at this point are not so clear, and the hints given in the Epistles do not help at all. It is a fact, however, that this was a period during which Paul laboured and found himself in danger, yet he founded churches at Colossi, Ierapolis, Laodikeia and elsewhere. After this, Paul chose to head for Greece. As the Acts state, Paul left for Macedonia and southern Greece, with a three-month sojourn in Corinth. It appears that he had made another sudden journey there previously. When he decided to set sail from Syria, a plot against him set his programme back and he preferred to follow an overland route, passing once more through Macedonia.

Along with Luke, they passed through central Greece as far as Philippi, from where they travelled to Troas. Here they were met by Sopater of Berea, Aristarchus and Secundus of Thessaloniki, Gaius of Derbe, Timothy, Tychicus and Trophimus. They stayed there for three days and Paul then went by road to Assos, a city of Asia Minor opposite Methymne, a fine port on the island of Lesbos known for the 'Assos stone' that the kings of Persia would buy.

The Hellenistic walls that have survived at nearby Kalloni, on the beach of the Kings, are in a very good condition. Paul's destination was Miletus.

MYTILENE - CHIOS - SAMOS

fter they left Assos they crossed over to Mytilene by boat, arriving at Chios the next day and continuing for Samos, where they stayed at Trogyllium (Acts 20:15). A journey of three days, all in all. Tradition holds that Paul's boat approached the gulf of Ephesus but bypassed it because Paul was in a hurry to reach Jerusalem for the Day of Pentecost.

When he mentions Mytilene the author of the Acts of course discusses the island of Lesbos, the largest city of which was Mytilene, the finest of the island's six cities and hometown of Pittakos the ruler. The oldest city remains date to the Middle Helladic years, and were built over the so-called 'island' of Kastro, with two very important natural lakes, one on the site of today's commercial port and the other further to the north.

The castle of Mytilene.

The little port at Molyvos.

Of Mytilene's archaeological monuments, the ancient theatre is particularly interesting, and is estimated to have had a seating capacity of 10,000. The so-called Menandron villa, dating to the 3rd century BC, has wonderful mosaics representing rare themes from the work of the comic playwright Menander and with Orpheus playing his lyre whilst being observed by enchanted animals. In our days, in addition to its rare natural beauty, this verdant island has much to offer the visitor, such as its fine neo-classical houses. It can also boast a number of saints and martyrs of the Orthodox church, of whom the best known are Saints Thermi, Raphael, Nikolaos and Irene. Their Monasteries attract crowds of worshippers.

1. The Orpheus octagon,
   mosaic from the Menandron villa.
2. Mansions of Lesbos and Ayios Therapontas.
3. The Monastery of Ayios Raphael at the height of Karyes.
4. Ruins of an early Christian basilica in the region
   of Halinados, near Ayia Paraskevi.

3

4

The island of Chios - also known in antiquity as Pityousa, Ophiousa, Aithale and Makris - is located at a perfect point in the Aegean. It is fertile and renowned for its mastic production. Chios town was one of the first cities in antiquity to use coinage for its exchange. In addition to its association with Homer, Chios was home to many leading cultural and intellectual figures, such as the thinker Ion, the philosopher Metrodoros, the sophist brothers Dionysodoros and Euthydemos, the poet Theocritus and the orator Likymnios. Sculptors from Chios include Acermos, Glaukos and Lysias. In the modern era, the tragic desolation of 1822 and the slaughter of its inhabitants shocked international public opinion. The painter Delacroix immortalised the event in his stunning painting, as did Victor Hugo in his poem 'L'enfant grec'.

As for Samos, this was a fine trading and maritime island of the Aegean, producing many brave seafarers, such as Kolaios, who travelled as far as the Gates of Herakles, today's Gibraltar, in around 600 BC. Samos also had many important colonies in different parts of the then known world, such as in Thrace, Cilicia and Egypt. Under the tyrant Polykrates (second half of the 6th century BC) it witnessed unique economic and artistic prosperity.

The Tunnel of Eupalinos, the famous temple of Hera, the mole of the port, described as "earth in sea" by Herodotus, and its fortress wall, are great achievements. Polykrates's clash with the Persians resulted in his death. An interesting historical detail to be noted is that the bridge over which the Persian army crossed the Hellespont was built by the Samian Androkles.

The Heraion, or temple of Hera, features eight successive levels, from the 3rd millennium to the 1st century BC, and there were numerous building phases in the historical years. The Iera Odos, or Sacred Way, linked the temple to the city, known today as Pythagorion. The Agora was located in the vicinity of the port, and around there were the Bouleuterion (Council), the Andron (banqueting hall), the Archive (in which the city's decrees were kept), Baths, Gymnasia, a theatre. These are just some of the ancient monuments that adorn the island. A plethora of early Christian basilicas gives witness to the early arrival of Christianity to Samos.

1, 2. Chios. Anavatos village and Pyrgi with the little church of the Theotokos.
3. The Heraion of Samos.

MILETUS - KOS - RHODES

iletus, homeland of Thales, Anaximander, Anaximenes, Hecataeus and so many other great figures of ancient civilisation, was a fine Ionian city built on an estuary of the Maeander river. Over the centuries, this river has left silt deposits of nine metres long, resulting in the creation of the city's four celebrated lakes, although these have now disappeared.

The area had been settled since Neolithic times, and Cretans, Myceneans, Karyans and Ionians later settled here. It played a leading role in the Ionian Rebellion and was levelled in 494 BC in retribution. A member of the first Athenian League, it later became a Spartan base and then passed to Persian rule, until it was liberated by Alexander the Great. In the Roman period it initially witnessed a decline, only to blossom again under Trajan and Marcus Aurelius.

In antiquity Samos was a particularly fine commercial centre, and its south Agora was the largest in the ancient Greek world that we know of today. Temples to Athens and Apollo, a Bouleuterion, Stadium, Gymnasium, Nymphaium, Baths and a particularly well-preserved theatre with a seating capacity of 15,000 and a view over the Aegean Sea are among the ancient city's most important monuments.

Saint Paul invited the Elders of the Church of Ephesus to Miletus, and greeted them saying that he did not know what might happen to him at Jerusalem. He emphasised that *"none of these things move me; nor do I count my life dear to myself, so that I may finish my race with joy, and the ministry which I received from the Lord Jesus, to testify to the gospel of the grace of God"* (Acts 20:24).

1. Theatre
2. Monument
3, 4. Lions
5. Roman baths
6. Old port
7. Synagogue
8. Port monument
9. Port Stoa
10. Delphinion
11. Port Gate
12. Small Agora
13. North Agora, classical period
14. Ionian Stoa
15. Iera Odos
16. Baths of Capitus
17. Gymnasium
18. Temple of Asklepios
19. Temple of Emperors
20. Bouleterion
21. Fountain
22. North Gate
23. Metropolitan church
24. North Agora, Hellenistic period
25. Storerooms
26. Monument
27. Temple of Serapis
28. Baths of Faustina

DIAGRAM OF ANCIENT MILETUS

The ancient theatre of Miletus, built in the 4th century AD with a seating capacity of 15,000.

The next day he continued on his journey, passing through Kos, reaching Rhodes the next day and from there on to Patara.

The city of Kos, built on the northeast edge of the island on a splendid commercial and military site, is located in an area that has been continuously occupied since the 3rd millennium BC. It was famed for its sanctuary of Asklepios, although no finds have been made at the archaeological site that would actually connect it with Asklepios. This is not the right place to go into further discussion of this matter, nor of the relationship between 'the Plane Tree of Hippocrates' with the famed doctor of antiquity. Tradition, nonetheless, holds that when he passed through Kos Saint Paul stopped and spoke with the people near this age-old plane tree, which is to be found near the Castle of the Knights and a Turkish fountain. The history of the town and island of Kos is long and complex, and its monuments, needless to say, spread out over a large area. What must be said, however, is that historical circumstance has proved favourable to this place, and it has been systematically investigated by Italian and Greek archaeologists, providing us with a substantially clear image of the island's development. The Agora, Odeion, House of Dionysus, the Baths, Stadium, Gymnasium, Nymphaion, early Christian basilicas, the Castle of the Knights are just a few of the island's most important monuments. In the capital, they form an integral part of the daily life of the inhabitants, being found commingled with modern buildings to create a charming whole that has made Kos a centre of attraction for many foreign visitors.

1. The temple of Apollo (sanctuary of Asklepios).
2. The plane tree of Hippokrates.
3. The ancient Agora.
4. View from the castle.

1

2

3

4

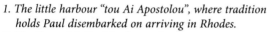

1. The little harbour "tou Ai Apostolou", where tradition
   holds Paul disembarked on arriving in Rhodes.
2. The Gate of St Paul in the castle.
3. The archaeological site of Lindos.
4. Interior of the church of the Panayia of Lindos.

On Rhodes tradition holds that Saint Paul's boat anchored at the small harbour of Lindos, in the south of the island. Lindos, set in an idyllic location in roughly the centre of the island's east coast, has been inhabited since the Late Neolithic period until today and makes for a charming archaeological site. In the modern village the church of the Panayia was built before the conquest of the island by the Knights and contains some particularly impressive wall paintings. It continues to express the religious zeal of its inhabitants, who abandoned their worship of Athena on the Acropolis and followed the sweet Nazarene, whose Gospel was brought to the island by the Apostle to the Gentiles. The little harbour at which Saint Paul disembarked at Lindos is referred to as 'tou Ai Apostolou', the Saint-Apostle's.

Passing Patara, Paul and his companions changed boats at Phoenicia and headed for Tyre. Here they met with disciples and stayed for seven days. The people here insisted to Paul that he should not continue on to Jerusalem, but he finally bid them and their wives and children goodbye. In the Acts of the Apostles it is poignantly noted that *"we knelt down on the shores and prayed. When we had taken our leave of one another, we boarded the ship and they returned home"*. They continued past Ptolemais, Caesarea and then reached Jerusalem.

Paul's teachings had outraged the Jews here, and when they saw him enter the Temple they caused such a riot that the chilarch, the army officer, ordered that he be taken to the barracks, be whipped and interrogated to provide an explanation of the outcry against him.

FOURTH MISSION (AD 59 - 61)
THE JOURNEY TO ROME

That night in AD 58 when the Lord appeared to Paul at the military barracks in Jerusalem and said to him, *"Be of good cheer, Paul; for as you have testified for Me in Jerusalem, so you must also bear witness at Rome"* (Acts 23:11), this is the night that Paul started upon his first journey for Rome. After the uproar at Jerusalem, the Apostle to the Gentiles was arrested and eventually led to the governor Felix at Caesarea, where he was kept under lock and key for two years. Felix's successor, Festus, sent Paul, as a Roman citizen, to be tried at Rome by the Emperor (Acts 25:12).

Paul's journey to Rome was episodic. They started in a boat that belonged to ship owners from Adramyttium, a city in the region of Troas in Asia Minor. They stopped at many ports that were on the ship's route, finally embarking upon an Alexandrian merchant ship that was sailing to Italy from Myra in Lycia. Sailing with difficulty because of the winds, they came to Cnidus, the capital of the Dorian Hexapolis with an important trading activity. The buildings that Cnidus had dedicated at Delphi, the Treasury and the Lesche (club house), indicate how wealthy the city was, something that is confirmed

by its two ports, which communicated via a canal. Many celebrated figures were born here, such as the geographer Eudoxos and the architect Sostratos who designed the Pharos lighthouse at Alexandria.

The strong winds meant that from Cnidus they found themselves to the south of Crete at Goodhaven - Kaloi Limenes. These are bays that lie on the south coast of today's Prefecture of Heraklion, which in the past few years have been developed into mooring spots with modern port facilities. Neither in the Acts nor in any other written source is mention made of a sojourn by Paul in Crete. In his Epistle to Titus, the Apostle does however state that he remained in Crete in order to see to some issues and install elders in each city (Tit. 1:5). This, however, is more likely to refer to another visit that Paul made to Crete, perhaps in AD 64, although this is not completely certain. Cretan tradition holds that Paul visited the city of Loutro, and there is a cave at Kaloi Limenes where it is said that he stayed.

Paul, seeing that the weather was worsening, advised that they stay there, but the captain preferred that they continue to Phoenix, another "harbour of Crete" that was safer, and to spend the winter there.

They set off with a wind that seemed to them fair, but its direction soon changed, the weather became wild and the wind turned into a Euryclodon, a storm from the east, which propelled them along without them being able to react. They travelled in unknown waters for days, without sun or stars and without knowing where they were going. They were forced to drop all the ship's cargo and tackle overboard, and sailed through the storm without hope or consolation. One morning Saint Paul said to them: *"There stood by me this night an angel of the God to whom I belong and whom I serve, saying, 'Do not be afraid, Paul; you must be brought before Caesar; and indeed God has granted you all those who sail with you'."* They remained at sea for fourteen days until they sensed that they were drawing near to land, and soon they came into a sandy bay. All two hundred and seventy-six souls on board were saved. It was the autumn of AD 59.

1. *The little church of St Paul.*
2. *The village of Loutro.*

MELITE

Argostoli, Cephalonia.

he inhabitants ran to help them and told them that they were on the island of Melite. They lit a fire to warm and dry the passengers. As Paul was gathering dry sticks and grass and putting them on the fire, a viper came out and bit his hand. All those around him froze, expecting to see him die from the horrific pain. But to everyone's great surprise, he suffered no harm.

A little further down from where they had been washed ashore was the house of Publius, the island's wealthiest and leading citizen, who had lain ill for days. Paul visited him, and laid his hands on his body, that was burning with fever, and prayed. Publius was cured. After this, everyone on the island who was ill ran to the Apostle to be cured. During their stay on Melite, the inhabitants showed them much love, supplying them with the necessary goods when they decided that the time had come to

leave. After a sojourn of three months on Melite, they embarked upon another Alexandrian boat and set sail for Italy.

Where exactly was this Melite, where, as the Acts of the Apostles show, Paul and all those who were travelling with him to Rome were saved?

The first effort to identify the island was made by the Byzantine Emperor Constantine Porphyrogennitos in the 10th century. In those days it was believed that the island today known as Mljet along the Dalmatian coast fulfilled all the historical criteria for the Melite of the Acts. The association of Malta with Melite dates to the 16th century, originating with the Knights of St John, who later became the Knights of Malta. Later, when Malta became a British naval base in the Mediterranean, the island was promoted as the Melite of the Acts, yet without there being sufficient evidence.

In 1987 the German scholar H. Warnecke, in a dissertation written at the Philosophical School of the University of Bremen, demonstrated scientifically that the Melite of the Acts of the Apostles is in fact Cephalonia, thus undermining positions and theories that had been put forward without real evidence. A brief discussion of Warnecke's treatise would prove useful at this point, focussing on a few of the obvious and logical points that he makes, which are scientifically proven from many perspectives.

Phoenix, the safe harbour sought by Paul's companions, is not to be found in Crete. It is in fact Phoinikounta, a leeward port to the east of Methoni on the southern edge of the Peloponnese. The fair south wind that they were waiting for confirms this view. The reference to Adria indicates the journey towards the north-west, the Adriatic, and not towards the Libyan Sea, where Malta lies.

The gulf where they disembarked, where the waves left them, is the gulf of Livadi, i.e. today's Argostoli, which in antiquity was always known as a safe military and commercial port. There is nothing of the kind in Malta. The fact that the site of the shipwreck was the seat of a distinguished personage of the island, Publius, also verifies that Cephalonia was the place. This was a region that had been inhabited since prehistoric times and where, indeed, lie the remains of ancient Kranioi, where the Roman officials were based from 189 BC until AD 395.

The snake that bit Paul belonged to the Tarbophis fallax family, which is not poisonous, and this is the reason why he suffered no harm. It must, however, be noted that there are many poisonous snakes on Cephalonia, unlike in Malta. Mention must also be made of the little snake that appears each year on the island on the festival of the Dormition of the Virgin, 15 August, and which is not poisonous.

Publius's illness (fever, dysentery, etc.) could not occur on Malta, which does not have hives of mosquitoes, unlike Cephalonia.

H. Warnecke, has provided much detailed evidence, too much to mention all of it here. What is of particular importance is that his proposition has been accepted by almost all specialist scholars.

At a short distance from Argostoli is the Convent of Agios Gerasimos, where this Saint's imperishable, intact and sweet smelling relic is kept. Saint Gerasimos died on 15 August 1579, but for the purposes of ecclesiastical economy his memory is honoured on 16 August. His hermitage survives in the church, and one can descend into it via a 3-metre long stairway, and which at one opening is divided into two 'rooms'. Three springs are preserved in the Convent of the miracle-working Saint, as well as the 37 smaller ones that he opened with his hands to bring water to the arid region. There are also two threshing floors that he himself constructed to provide the necessary foodstuffs to the nuns of the Convent that he himself founded, with the little chapel of the Dormition of the Virgin (1560).

ROME - THE END

he journey passed as normal from Melite. The Apostle to the Gentiles stayed here in private accommodation with his escort. In his speeches to the Jews of Rome he explained the reasons why he was brought there in chains and preached the Kingdom of Heaven. Some believed his words, others did not. The Acts of the Apostles end at this point and with these words: *"Then Paul dwelt two whole years in his own rented house, and received all who came to him, preaching the kingdom of God and teaching the things which concern the Lord Jesus Christ with all confidence, no one forbidding him."* (Acts 28:30-31).

In chronological terms, his first visit to Rome is dated to AD 60-61 and his first imprisonment to 61-63. It has been said that the day on which Paul entered Rome was one of the greatest days in history. It is from this day that the tradition that Eirenaios discusses, i.e. that the Church of Rome was founded by the two Apostles Peter and Paul, is deemed to begin. The year of his first imprisonment in Rome was one of the Saint's most fruitful years. It was well worth the effort, because Christianity managed to penetrate further and further into the Roman army, through the praetorian guards who travelled to all the parts of the known world, the Rhine, France, Britain and Spain. Most of all, this is where Paul's theology fully matured, along with his mystic vision of the eternal Christ and of the head of the Church.

Saint Paul's epistle to the Romans features certain problems regarding history and content. According to Renan it appears to have been a circular which, with a different ending, was sent to various recipients, and was written in Corinth before his journey to Rome. Its purpose was to make advance preparations for his arrival in Rome and his subsequent campaign in Spain. *"Now I do not want you to be unaware, brethren, that I often planned to come to you (but was hindered until now), that I might have some fruit among you also, just as among the other Gentiles. I am a debtor both to Greeks and to barbarians, both to wise and unwise. So, as much as is in me, I am ready to preach the gospel to you who are in Rome also"* (Romans 1:13-15).

1. *The Coliseum.*
2. *The Roman Forum.*

1

2

What exactly happened after Saint Paul was released from his first imprisonment in Rome is now known. It appears that he made a journey to the western borders, and ancient tradition holds that he was imprisoned once more in Rome under Nero, to be released again during the persecution of the Christians.

The decapitation of the Apostle to the Gentiles is described in four apocryphal works: a) the Acta Pauli, written in Greek, b) the Passio S. Pauli apostoli, written in Latin, c) the Acts of the Apostles Peter and Paul, in Greek, and d) the Martyrdom of Peter and Paul, in Greek and Latin. According to the Apocryphal tradition, then, the Apostle Paul was beheaded at Aquae Salviae, a little outside Rome at the spot today known as Tre Fontane, because at the points at which the Saint writhed three times three springs gushed out. The area belongs to the Abbazia delle Tre Fontanae of the Trappist Monks. A church was built on this site in the 5th century, being rebuilt at the end of the 16th century. It is even said that Paul had been tied during his execution to the column that stands between the two Holy Tables of the church.

1. View of the interior of the basilica of St Paul outside the walls.
2. The Appian Way.
3. Catacomb of St Sebastian.

2   Some Christians buried the dead Paul at a spot three miles from the site of his martyrdom on the farm of the Roman woman Lucine, where the church of San Paolo fuori le Mura stands today in a simple crypt. His relic remained there until the era of Valerian in the 3rd century, when they were moved, along with those of Saint Peter, to the catacombs of St Sebastian along the Appian Way, so as to be protected from being destroyed in the manic persecution of the Christians. The bones of the great Apostles were returned to their original position by Pope Sylvester, into the churches that were built by the Emperor Constantine the Great. A little later the great basilica of Saint Paul was 3 built, this splendid building being completed in the late 4th century. This church survived until 1823, when it was destroyed in a fire.

Early Christian sculpture as it appears on various works of art, in particular sarcophagi, has as a theme the beheading of Saint Paul. Mention was made of these *sarcophagi passionis* at the beginning of the book. We shall again note the most representative of these works, the sarcophagus of Junius Bassus in the Grotte Vaticane in Rome, and consider it from another view. It is a work of great importance for Christian art in general, both from a stylistic perspective as well as the fact that it is one of the few sarcophagi to survive for which we have a precise date. On its long sides there are two series with scenes from the Old and New Testaments, divided by colonettes. One of these scenes depicts the process of the fatal execution. In the centre of the scene stands Saint Paul, dressed in chiton and himation, his hands bound behind him and with a slight tilt of the head, framed by two soldiers one of whom is preparing to draw his sword from its sheath. The reeds seen in between the soldier and the Apostle represent the marshy land of the Aquae salviae. A similar scene is shown on the sarcophagus of St Sebastian in Rome, where only one solder is represented.

It has been observed that the manner in which Saint Paul is represented, and which has come down to us from early Christian sculpture, is not a precise portrayal of the beheading of the great Apostle. We can learn much, however, from the presence of the executioner attempting to draw his sword from its sheath or of other soldiers tying the rope around the martyr's neck or standing as guards. The existence of reeds in a marsh even, or of a small boat on a column, the appearance of a female figure identifiable as Thekla or Plautilla, provide powerful iconographic details that fit the details given in the Apocryphal writings, to give a symbolic representation of the beheading of Saint Paul. In other words, what is missing from the known historical sources helps to fill in the pieces to give a comprehensive picture of the last days of Saint Paul in Rome.

Christ between Saints Peter and Paul.
Sculpture on a sarcophagus, 15th century, Vatican.

Right: Saint Paul. Detail from a wall painting in the Monastery of St Dionysios, Mount Athos.

BIBLIOGRAPHY

ΖΗΚΟΥ Ν.: *Αμφίπολη, Παλαιοχριστιανική και Βυζαντινή Αμφίπολη*, Athens 1989.

ΛΑΖΑΡΙΔΗ Δ., *Νεάπολις, Χριστούπολις, Καβάλα*, Οδηγός Μουσείου Καβάλας, 1969.

ΜΑΞΙΜΟΣ ΠΛ., *Αρχαία Ελληνικά Θέατρα, 2.500 χρόνια φως και πνεύμα*, Athens 1998.

ΜΑΣΤΡΑΠΑ Ν. Α., *Μνημειακή Τοπογραφία της Αρχαίας Αθήνας*, editions Καρδαμίτσας, Athens 1992.

ΜΑΤΣΑ Δ. - ΜΠΑΚΙΡΤΖΗ Α., *Σαμοθράκη*, Μικρός Πολιτισμικός Οδηγός, Athens 2001.

ΜΕΤΑΛΛΗΝΟΥ Γ., πρωτοπρεσβυτέρου, *Ο Απόστολος Παύλος στην Κεφαλληνία*, Athens 1993.

ΟΡΛΑΝΔΟΥ Αν., *Η ξυλόστεγη Παλαιοχριστιανική βασιλική της Μεσογειακής Λεκάνης*, τ. Α΄ Athens 1952.

ΠΑΠΑΣΤΑΥΡΟΥ Ι., *Ρωμαϊκή Ιστορία*, Athens 1967.

ΠΑΥΛΙΔΗ Α., ΓΙΑΣΕΜΙΔΗ Σ., *Πάφος, πόλη και επαρχία*, editions Φιλόκυπρος, Λευκωσία 1987.

ΠΑΥΣΑΝΙΟΥ *Ελλάδος Περιήγησις*, μετ. επιμ. κ.λπ. Παπαχατζή Ν. editions Εκδοτική Αθηνών.

ΠΡΟΚΟΠΙΟΥ, Μητροπολίτου Φιλίππων, Νεαπόλεως και Θάσου, *Από-στολος Παύλος και Φίλιπποι, Το βαπτιστήριο της Αγίας Λυδίας*, editions Αναπτυξιακή Καβάλα Α.Ε., 1η έκδοση, Καβάλα 1994.

ΣΛΗΜΑΝ Ερ., *Ανταποκρίσεις από την Τροία*, editions Ωκεανίδα 2000.

ΣΩΤΗΡΙΟΥ Γ., *Χριστιανική και Βυζαντινή Αρχαιολογική*, τ. Α΄ *Χριστιανικά Κοιμητήρια, Εκκλησιαστική Αρχιτεκτονική*, Athens 1942.

ΤΑΛΙΑΝΗ Δ. - ΣΕΡΕΛΗ Κ., *Ες Κύπρον*, Εκδόσεις Τοπίο, Αθήνα

ΤΣΟΥΝΤΑ Χρ., *Ιστορία της Αρχαίας Ελληνικής Τέχνης*, editions Τοξότης 1965.

ΦΥΛΑΚΤΟΥ Κ. Α., *Πάφος*, Τουριστικός Οδηγός, Λευκωσία 1978.

ΧΑΤΖΗΦΩΤΗ Ι. Λ., *Τα βήματα του Αποστόλου Παύλου στην Ελλάδα*, editions Ε.Ο.Τ., Athens 2003.

ΧΑΤΖΗΦΩΤΗ Ι. Μ., Μακεδονική Σχολή, *Η Σχολή του Πανσέληνου* (1290-1320), Athens 1995.

ΑΠΟΣΤΟΛΟΣ ΠΑΥΛΟΣ, editions Αποστολική Διακονία, Athens 2000.

"ΕΠΤΑΠΥΡΓΙΟ, η Ακρόπολη της Θεσσαλονίκης", στη σειρά *Ώρες Βυζαντίου, έργα και ημέρες στο Βυζάντιο*, Υπουργείο Πολιτισμού, Athens 2001.

ΗΡΟΔΟΤΟΥ ΙΣΤΟΡΙΑΙ, τ. Α´ (Α-Β), μετ. Άγγ. Βλάχου, editions Παπαδήμας, 2η έκδοση, Athens 1978.

Η ΘΕΣΣΑΛΟΝΙΚΗ ΚΑΙ ΤΑ ΜΝΗΜΕΙΑ ΤΗΣ, Εφορία Βυζαντινών Αρχαιοτήτων Θεσσαλονίκης, Θεσσαλονίκη 1985 (όπου και περαιτέρω εκτενής βιβλιογραφία).

Η ΚΑΙΝΗ ΔΙΑΘΗΚΗ, editions Βιβλικής Εταιρείας, 1985.

"ΘΕΣΣΑΛΟΝΙΚΗ", (Από τα προϊστορικά μέχρι τα χριστιανικά χρόνια) *Οδηγός έκθεσης* αφιερωμένης στα 2300 χρόνια, Αρχαιολογικό Μουσείο Θεσσαλονίκης, Athens 1986 (όπου και περαιτέρω εκτενής βιβλιογραφία).

ΜΑΝΟΥΗΛ ΠΑΝΣΕΛΗΝΟΣ, ΕΚ ΤΟΥ ΙΕΡΟΥ ΝΑΟΥ ΤΟΥ ΠΡΩΤΑΤΟΥ, editions Αγιορείτικη Εστία, Θεσσαλονίκη 2003.

ΘΟΥΚΥΔΙΔΟΥ ΙΣΤΟΡΙΑ, τ. Α´ (Ι-IV), editions Οξφόρδης, 1966.

ΘΡΗΣΚΕΥΤΙΚΗ ΚΑΙ ΗΘΙΚΗ ΕΓΚΥΚΛΟΠΑΙΔΕΙΑ, λήμμα "Παύλος", Athens 1963.

Ι. Μ. ΘΕΣΣΑΛΟΝΙΚΗΣ, *Απόστολος Παύλος, Πρακτικά Θεολογικού Συνεδρίου* 1987, Θεσσαλονίκη 1989.

Ι. Μ. ΚΕΦΑΛΛΗΝΙΑΣ, *Σύντομος Προσκυνηματικός Οδηγός*, 1997.

ΙΣΤΟΡΙΑ ΤΟΥ ΕΛΛΗΝΙΚΟΥ ΈΘΝΟΥΣ, editions Εκδοτική Αθηνών, Αθήνα *ΠΑΝΗΓΥΡΙΚΟΣ ΤΟΜΟΣ* Εορτασμού της 1900ης Επετείου της Ελεύσεως του Απ. Παύλου εις την Ελλάδα, Athens 1953.

ΡΩΜΗ, από τις απαρχές ως το 2000, οδηγός,
CYPRUS, a civilization plundered, Έκδοση της Βουλής των Ελλήνων, Athens 2000.

BLEGEN W.: C. Troy, 1963.

DELVOYE Ch.: *Βυζαντινή Τέχνη*, editions Παπαδήμας, Athens 1991.

GUNNEWEG H.J.A.: *Η Ιστορία του Ισραήλ έως την εξέγερση του Βαρ-Κόχβα*, editions Π. Πουρναράς, Θεσσαλονίκη 1997.

HOLZNER J.: *Παύλος*, (μετάφραση Ιερ. Ι. Κωτσώνη), editions Δαμασκός, Αθήνα.

ILHAN Akşit: *Ancient Treasures of Turkey*, Istanbul 1987.

LEWIS P.: *Syria, Land of Contrasts*, London 1980.

ΒΕΡΔΕΛΗ Ν.: *Der Dioklos am Isthmus von Korinth*, Ath. Mitt. 1965.

Text: LITSA I. HADJIFOTI
Artistic editor: EVI DAMIRI
Translation: DESPINA CHRISTODOULOU
Photographs: M. TOUBIS SA ARCHIVE

Printing- production: M. TOUBIS S.A.